New Inn Entry Office, 1808.

"Advertiser" Office, Church Lane, 1802.

Argyle Close, 1838.

Bank Street, 1859.

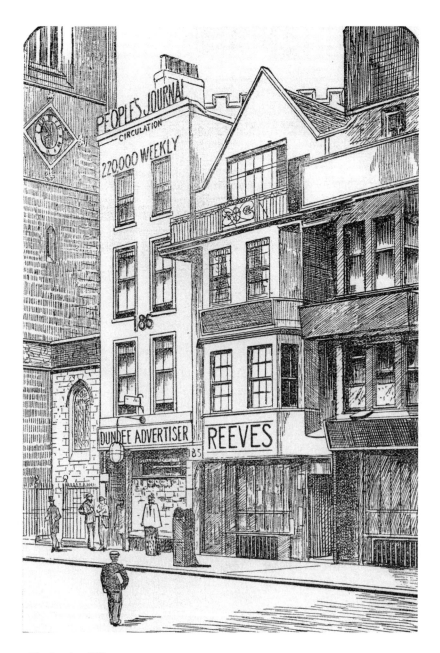

The London Office.

THE LENGS
DUNDEE'S OTHER PUBLISHING DYNASTY

by
Gordon Small

Sir JOHN LENG.
(FROM PHOTOGRAPH TAKEN IN 1851)

Published by The Tay Valley Family History Society
Printed by D.C. Thomson & Co Ltd.

INTRODUCTION

THIS is the story of a Dundee-based publishing house which, when it functioned as an independent firm between 1851 and 1905, changed the face of periodicals in Scotland, and became a market leader and innovator in UK terms. It was vigorous and pioneering.

The firm did not pay only lip-service to radicalism. The proprietors believed in it, fought hard for social change, and in this, were successful. The publications became a platform for the advancement of the worth of the Scottish way of life, which spread not only south of the border but to the farthest reaches of the Commonweath.

John Leng & Co. Ltd made Scottish journalism truly professional in a way it had never been before. It moved the hub of Scottish journalism to Dundee, far ahead of other Scottish cities, and enlarged the influence which newspapers had over the working classes in Scotland like no other company had done before. The weekly *People's Journal* was eagerly awaited all over Scotland and beyond.

The titles which the firm published were much loved and respected, and they were survivors.

All this happened through the drive and ability of an Englishman who came to Dundee in 1851.

This remarkable gentleman was John Leng.

FOREWORD

AS a Morgan schoolboy, around 1947, I was standing in the queue at Tannadice Park to watch my beloved United. A tall gentleman in a soft hat and a long raincoat singled me out and announced that he was George McIntosh, the local reporter for *The Glasgow Herald*. He wondered if I would care to be his assistant at football matches?

I leapt at the chance and in Dundee parlance, I felt I was Erchie. I got a Press pass for Dens and Tannadice, a seat in the Press Box and five bob as recompense. All I had to do for this munificence was to dash to the phone under the grandstand every 20 minutes or so, and phone Mr. McIntosh's copy to Glasgow.

This was a lesson in geography. Firstly, you dialled zero for the operator, who put you through to Perth. Another to Stirling and a third to Denny. Finally I got through to the *Herald*. The first time I did it, a man kept yelling "Copy" at me. I had no idea what he was talking about, but of course he was the man who typed up the "copy" and I soon got the hang of it. It was so exciting, I was one of the Press and the envy of all my pals.

Eventually, I reported on important Junior matches and when Mr. McIntosh was on holiday, I did the job at Dens and Tannadice. I must have got the bug at that time.

After two years National Service as an unlikely RAF jet engine mechanic, my father, who was the city's Chief Librarian and "kent a'body" in Dundee, fixed me up with an interview with J.B. Hood, the editor of *The People's Journal.* I started there in October 1954, on the precise day that the great D.C. Thomson was spirited away by the angels. I always thought that the prospect of me joining his illustrious company was too much for the old boy.

Bank Street was a warren of old buildings and had been the headquarters of John Leng and Company, taken over by D.C. Thomson in 1905.

The Journal was a great training ground and I looked forward to going to work every day and being involved. Things moved at a brisk pace and there was a constant stir. Every Friday at 11 o'clock there was an editorial conference, where you had to come up with ideas for stories and features. Jimmy Hood was in charge and all the ideas got an airing. Some were proceeded with, some were rejected and some were modified. In this way, you learned the ropes.

It was a wonderful training procedure and I adopted it for all the other papers I controlled eventually. It was one of the reasons that Thomson journalists could get a job anywhere at that time.

With hindsight, the commercial regime which ran Bank Street, as opposed to the editorial, didn't follow Leng's liberal attitudes. There seemed to be a lot of bosses, or people who wanted to be bosses. You always felt a bit under undeserved scrutiny. So definitely not Liberal. Also, there was a funny disinfectant smell about the place.

The Thomson family themselves were always gentlemanly and polite. The resident director in Bank Street was the tall and spare Sidney Thomson who had won the Military Cross in the first world war.

The Chairman, and Mr Sidney's brother, Mr W. Harold Thomson, came in most days to see Jimmy Hood. Mr Harold was a tall, well-built man who had a kind of permanent tan. He wore a raincoat that had seen better days and a battered soft hat. He carried a non-rolled umbrella and a battle-scarred briefcase. His appearance and manner were benign and this was accentuated by his half-round spectacles. He was brimful of enthusiasm and ideas. He would suggest all manner of things and leave some kind of chaos behind him. John Martin (the editor) and Mr. WHT were largely responsible for the success of *The Sunday Post,* at that time the biggest-selling newspaper per head of population in the world.

Later, when we were seeking a title for a new teenage paper which I created and was to edit, eventually called *Jackie*, we had a series of meetings. All the top brass were there and I felt just a bit intimidated. Sitting next to WHT didn't help. I had drawn up a list of possible titles for the paper which were kicked around. Eventually, WHT came up with one of his own, "Cascade". This wasn't very good, but how to get him off it? I said "That's very good, Mr. Harold, but how about so and so?" Fortunately he let his idea drop. But he wasn't often wrong.

In 1956, I was transferred to Meadowside, seen by people there as the "head office." This was the Thomson building, opened in 1906. D.C. Thomson himself was very conservative and so you would think that he would leave a restricting legacy. Not so.

Meadowside was completely different from Bank Street. It was much bigger, and although over 50 years old, seemed modern. It had been built at one go, as a complete publishing house. Bank Street had been built piecemeal. Meadowside was lightsome, the stairs and corridors were wider, there were many more publications, a big art department and above all, lots of fun. You were aware of the eye of the general management, but the editorial were generally able to hoodwink them.

At that time, the publications were hugely successful and new ones were starting often. There was a buzz and morale was high. Among the magazine editorial, joy was unconfined.

The place was full of characters. People who played the accordion in working hours.

Others who played cricket in the corridor. Many who dreamed up practical jokes. A blind eye was turned to this provided we didn't go over the score. The reason for this tolerance was that, editorially, we knew what we were about and nobody dared to interfere. We sold papers. Lots of them. It was indeed a boom time.And the Meadowside disinfectant was so pleasant, you could (almost) have used it for aftershave.

Although I had my management offices at both Kingsway and Meadowside eventually, the latter was always home to me and I had some editorial success there. I retired in 1998 after almost 44 years service. I look back on almost all of it with enormous pleasure.

In 2004, the directors invited me to write a history of D.C. Thomson & Co for presentation to shareholders at the AGM that November. I felt proud to be asked and they in turn did me proud, with the best of paper and each copy being bound in beautiful sheepskin from the Pentland Hills. The book was never put on sale, and went to shareholders only. The print run was about 400.

In the preparation of that book, I came to know a bit about the Leng family. D.C.Thomson's brother William had married John Leng's daughter Clara and so the Lengs came into the Thomson story.

The Lengs, and particularly John Leng and his brother William, seemed very interesting and colourful people. I promised myself that one day I would write about them in book form. This is the result.

John Leng and all of his employees are long gone and the material I have written has been compiled from his own writings and musings, brochures published over the 50-odd years of his tenure, his many speeches, reports of company social functions and enterprises, a study of the newspapers of the period, some minor sources and from my own knowlege. I also had access to material in the local history library.

Gordon Small
Newport on Tay
December 2009

The Dundee Advertiser office 1802.

CONTENTS

*This is the type of hand-fed press used to print
early editions of The Advertiser.*

*Robert Rintoul, who edited The
Advertiser for 14 years from 1811 and
went on to found The Spectator*

CHAPTER 1

SETTING THE SCENE

IN order to appreciate the impact of John Leng's arrival on the Dundee newspaper scene, it is necessary to have an overview of what had happened before, both in the town, and also in the country as a whole. For the first 50 years of its life, Dundee's *Advertiser* was little different from the many newspapers which came and went in Scotland in the last quarter of the 18th century and the first half of the 19th.

The *'tiser*, as it became known in Dundee, was not very big, perhaps only four pages, the printing paper had a strong resemblance to cloth, and there were big gaps on the pages. Type was not always legible. Publication was sporadic, sometimes weekly, or twice or thrice per week at best. The paper was made from rags, for wood pulp didn't come into use until much later.

The editor generally worked alone in cramped premises, processing the work of contributors who lived within the circulation area. Type-setting was all done by hand, letter by letter, a laborious business indeed. Printing was usually farmed out on a contract basis to a local man who fed his press by hand, sheet by sheet.

Distribution was a continuing problem. In town, papers were mainly sold on street corners, and vendors took most of the profit. There were few roads outside the towns, only tracks and sometimes pack horses were used.

So the early newspapers had great difficulty in establishing anything like a healthy circulation, even in the towns. For another thing, because of taxation, they were relatively expensive.

Revenue largely depended on advertisements and most papers stumbled from one financial crisis to another.

Attempts had been made in Dundee in 1777 and 1799 to establish a monthly magazine which would also give some local news, but these were not successful.

The Dundee Weekly Advertiser was started by a Dundee surgeon, Robert Stewart. He obtained the necessary capital, and hired an efficient editor, James Roger. The paper was launched from an office in New Inn Entry - near the present Reform Street - on Friday 16 January 1801. Friday was good publication day, it still is. Weekends give people time to read and appreciate.

It cost sixpence and had eight pages, 13 inches by 10, three columns per page. By June of that year it went up to 21 by 14 inches and four columns per page. For the first 50 years of its life, the *Advertiser* was not any more viable than other Scottish papers, but it did survive. Eventually Stewart acquired an estate in Fife and moved away.

He was a radical and his paper reflected that political view from its launch, except for one nine-year period. After the General Strike in 1926, it amalgamated with the Tory *Courier,* both papers by then being owned by D.C. Thomson & Co.

The third editor requires mention. Robert Rintoul was born at Tibbermore in Perthshire in 1787, being educated at the parish school. Apprenticed to a printer, he eventually came to Dundee and *The Advertiser*.

In 1826, he went to London and in 1828 founded *The Spectator*, which is now the oldest continuously published magazine in the English language. True to his *Advertiser* beginnings, Rintoul was a radical and a strong supporter of the 1832 Reform Act (aimed at giving more people the vote). His catch phrase was "The Bill, the whole Bill, and nothing but the Bill".

He conducted *The Spectator* for more than 30 years, selling it shortly before his death in 1858.

CHAPTER 2

JOHN LENG'S EARLY YEARS

A DAM Leng, John Leng's father, had seen active service in the Royal Navy in the Mediterranean and the Baltic. He then settled in business in Hull without much success. He married Mary, daughter of Christopher Lucock, an architect, surveyor and estate agent who lived in Malton in the East Riding. Leng reports that both of his parents came from families that had "seen better days." There was never much money.

Adam and Mary had two boys, William Christopher and John. John was born on 10 April 1828 and William three years earlier. He too became a journalist of note, was knighted, and we will read more about him later.

There was also a daughter, Anne, who was born on 14 December 1819 and died on 14 August 1859. She married John Whiteley, a captain in the navy. Both she and her husband died early, leaving three orphan boys. Leng reports that "the boys remain in our care." There was another sister, Mary. She was baptized in Hull on 26 February 1826 and died in infancy.

Adam brought up his children in sailor-like activity, with the accent on punctuality and discipline. The boys' chief delight was in building and sailing model ships. They also spent a lot of time at Hull docks. This interest was almost the death of young John. One dark night, at high tide, he fell into the harbour and went under several times. An oar was thrown and a small boat launched. The men spotted him because of his white collar, and he was fished out.

John said that he was always small and delicate but that his brother was his strong protector. His health was such that it wasn't thought desirable to keep him on at school. During holidays, he was sent to an aunt in Scarborough for the sea air and bathing. He said later "The grandeur and mystery of the sea worshipped by me when a boy, filled me with sentiments of reverence which has helped to uphold me through life.

"I attribute the fair degree of health I had through life to the many happy days I spent on the cliffs at Scarborough." But he was never robust. In old age he looked back and said he wasn't expected to live to 50. He was always ailing and frequently overtaxed his strength.

If his father supplied the discipline, his mother encouraged creativity. Leng wrote- "My mother was a highly intelligent, quick-witted, warm-tempered, anxious, careful woman.

"She could rhyme and write, speak and pray with remarkable fluency. My brother and I got this from her. William was more poetical. He was imaginative and illustrative. I was more practical."

There was no money to send the boys to university, nor bursaries to help. But Leng didn't hide his light under a bushel. "Undoubtedly, I could have gone to Oxford or Cambridge," he said later.

John went to the local grammar school where he gained distinction as a keen scholar and a voracious reader. Later, he said he couldn't remember a time when he couldn't read and that the size of his forehead was often remarked upon. One day, the master mistook him for a miscreant and caned him severely. His mother, festering over this injustice, took him away and put him to a private school where he became a monitor, read the prayers and filled in the register when the master was late.

He used to go for the daily paper and read the salient points to his father before the paper was passed on to the next family. When quite young, perhaps about nine, he took part in debates, and could quote from various sources. He became known as "Lawyer Leng." Leng's mother wanted him to be a clergyman. On Sunday afternoons in the house, he would often dress up as a minister. She also saw him as a doctor. Alarmingly, he used to dispense medicines to his school friends.

But early on, in Hull, he showed a bent for journalism, acting as joint editor with a friend, Charles Cooper, of a magazine which was circulated among scholars. Cooper eventually became editor of *The Scotsman* and was one of Leng's referees when he applied for the Dundee job.

After leaving Hull Grammar School, his mother got him a job in a grocer's but he didn't linger. He took a job with an estate agent, and the chief attraction there was that they had a large library. He spent a year there, mainly just reading.

Next, he became an assistant teacher in a private school about which he said "dealing with stupid boys is a daily affliction."

He started to write occasional letters to Edward Collins, editor of *The Hull Advertiser*, a leading Liberal and radical provincial paper of the time. Collins was of Irish extraction and had been in London for a spell, where he mixed with leading radicals. He had worked on *The Sun* (not the present one), a powerful daily paper which urged radical reforms. All this experience he eventually passed on to Leng and this perhaps augmented and expanded the young man's own natural liberal and radical leanings.

Collins liked Leng's material and invited him along for a chat. Leng was somewhat taken aback to find his host wearing a long silk dressing gown and a crimson smoking cap. He looked like a wizard.

Lending Leng a book on journalism and encouraging him to study shorthand, the editor promised the lad a junior post on the paper when he had mastered the basic skills. Leng became proficient in shorthand and the other basic skills in three months. Referring later in life to the period which followed, John Leng wrote-

"I took pride in writing the best paragraphs of local news that appeared in any of the local papers. The man I assisted being an indolent, self-indulgent, tippling fellow, was glad to be relieved of the greater part of the work. Because he knew that I could be trusted not to neglect anything , he grew more and more negligent, and his habit became so disreputable that he was soon dismissed. At the age of 19, I was appointed sub-editor and reporter of the leading weekly paper in Hull". This was in 1847.

Leng found himself in at the deep end, and he revelled in it. Not only did he help to put the Hull weekly paper together in a practical way, he was the chief reporter, the drama critic, and the music critic – all valuable experience which would serve him well. He immersed himself in these matters for four years.

And then in 1851, two things happened which were to change his life. On the first day of October, he married Emily Cook at Beverley Minster. She was the elder daughter of the late Alderman Cook of Beverley and a distant relative of the famous Captain Cook.

And secondly, his attention was drawn to Advert No 471 in *The North British Advertiser*, published in Edinburgh. People up in Dundee were looking for an editor. Despite just being offered a seven-year contract at Hull, he had been feeling for some time the need to move on. Earlier in 1851, he had applied for a job on *The Inverness Advertiser* but didn't get it.

CHAPTER 3

GO NORTH, YOUNG MAN!

THE main owners of *The Dundee Advertiser* (strictly speaking, the title was *The Dundee, Perth and Cupar Advertiser* until 1861 when it became a daily paper) were two Dundee lawyers, James Pattullo and William Neish.

Pattullo and Neish, as part of a syndicate, had bought the paper at auction around 1850 for £800. They were associated with a Mr. Shaw, a bookseller, who was to market the paper. At one point, some early newspapers were distributed by lawyers who sent letters and missives on a regular basis to clients in surrounding areas. The newspapers went along too – a nice little earner for the men of the law. But the owners soon realized that the incumbent editor was the wrong man for the job.

Francis Willoughby Baxter, a lawyer, was related to William Baxter, founder of Baxter Brothers of Dundee who eventually owned the biggest flax mill in Europe, still there in Princes Street.

Francis had become editor in 1842. He had made a smart move by marrying Margaret Saunders whose father, also a Dundee lawyer, had edited the paper (unsuccessfully) but retained a financial interest for many years. During the early years of Baxter's editorship there was plenty to write about. The Free Kirk was formed following the 1843 Disruption, the Corn Laws were repealed, and Queen Victoria and Prince Albert visited Dundee.

But after that, things quietened down and the paper became more "gentlemanly". More literature, more theatre, less politics, less vigour.

But Dundee wasn't that kind of town. It wanted political fire and brimstone, and so sales fell away. The owners got rid of Baxter in March 1851 and a lawyer called John Austin Gloag took over. He had no idea of how to edit and even worse for the readership, he was a Conservative.

At that point, Neish and Pattullo, that part of the owning syndicate charged with legal matters, cried enough, fired Gloag, and advertised for an editor. They got 60-70 replies, one of them from John Leng.

He did a big sell in his opening correspondence with Pattullo in April 1851. His letters are still in Dundee Local History Library. Truthfully, he wrote that he had run the Hull operation almost single-handed. That he had amassed a library of over 200 reference books.

John Leng in his prime.

He laid out his ideas of how a weekly newspaper should be run. And more importantly, he told Pattullo that he was already on £120 a year and would only move if he got £150.

Considerable correspondence followed in which both men got a feel for each other's point of view. There was an interview in May at which terms were fixed and the first edition which Leng edited was on the streets on 8 July 1851.

When John Leng's new wife arrived in Dundee, they set up house in Springfield, off Perth Road. One of the Neishes, Captain James, who brought the original jute samples to Dundee, lived round the corner in Airlie Place.

In 1856, the Lengs had moved to 8 Craigie Terrace off Broughty Ferry Road, and before the Kinbrae mansion in Newport was built, he lived in Wellgate House, Newport. This white harled house is still there on the river side of the main road between Newport and Wormit, just east of Castle Brae. He rented it from St Fort estate.

Upon arrival in Dundee, Leng was faced with a problem with the content and his brief was to turn the paper round.

The printing facilities probably weren't any better or worse than many elsewhere. It was said that in the early 1800s, for instance, that a Dundee printer disposed of a press which had been used to do "wanted" notices for Prince Charles Edward Stuart after the '45 Uprising.

The *Advertiser* office was in Argyll Close, described as a "dingy and inconvenient spot" off the north side of the Overgate. Leng found himself with a very basic sheet-fed press worked by two men, plus a skilled printer and two apprentices. The output would be around 350 copies per hour. Each sheet had to be printed separately. In the machine room and type-setting departments, there were ten journeymen and eight apprentices. Leng tells of having the entire office staff, with the exception of the apprentices, round for supper in the small dining room of his house in Springfield.

Reminiscing at his Jubilee dinner in 1901, he said that in 1851 the holidays were few, the hours long and the wages (including his own) small. The total weekly wage bill was around £17. The solitary reporter, who was excellent at shorthand, was on one pound, seven shillings a week (£1.35). No wonder that he emigrated to Australia!

The type fonts and all the machinery had been run down through neglect and lack of investment. Leng's first task was to improve this situation. At that time, and through the following decades, he was to invest in the most up-to-date machinery and techniques. In this respect, he was always ahead of the game, and at the forefront of printing equipment. In December 1851, he installed a new press, and a new font of type.

Three years later a water-engine supplied the motive power instead of the manual labour used previously.

Because of the wide experience gained in Hull, Leng knew exactly what he had to do. The editorial content was greatly improved and the literary quality raised, so that the struggling paper which had lacked the teeth to challenge municipal affairs became a powerful exponent of public opinion.

His life-long crusade of righting wrongs started in a parochial way. The Public Seminaries, the direct original of the present High School, couldn't raise funds to pay competent teachers. In his first leader column, Leng advocated the endowment of classical and mathematical teachers at the school. The idea was implemented quickly, with remarkable results.

He objected to the Dundee Harbour Board's plan to hold a separate police court. Mind you, the harbour was always a place apart. As late as the 1960s, Dundee City Police was wont to send bobbies who had transgressed to work at the harbour as a penance. One ex-sergeant who is known to me often spent his summer night shift in mid-river, tunic off, fishing from a coble. So harbour service wasn't all bad!

Several of Leng's early campaigns are almost all lost in the mists of time, including support for the Edinburgh Angus Club which is still giving bursaries to able students today.

But his radical eye was already picking up on bigger matters further afield. After studying the 1851 census, he drew attention to what was going on in Ireland – a subject he would return to on a much wider stage as a Liberal MP when the question of Irish Home Rule was a hot issue.

Shortly after Leng took over, the Crimean war broke out. He introduced a series of supplements giving the latest war news. When the Indian Mutiny began, it too was reported upon.

His interest in furthering radical and liberal causes, which also appealed to the core of his readership, was enhanced by what was going on in national politics. This gave him lots of things to write about. His independent and liberal attitude, established in his early editorial days, was maintained throughout his active work as leader writer for *The Advertiser*. He never lost that invaluable and inbred quality of the successful editor – a warm and engaging rapport with his readers.

As the administrative side of the business increased, he wrote less himself, but he suggested subjects to his assistants and completely supervised the content of *The Advertiser*, and all the character and quality of all the publications he launched subsequently.

Great parliamentary battles between the three Prime Ministers - Palmerston, Derby and Russell – rolled on into the time of Leng's arrival. Derby, particularly, sang from the same song sheet as Leng, and Derby's perseverance led to the passing of the Reform Bill of 1832. Derby introduced civil registrations of births, marriages and deaths and reduced the number of offences to which corporal punishment was applicable.

Russell – and Leng – had great sympathy for the poor. Russell wrote "What a pity that he who steals a penny loaf should be hung, while he who steals thousands of the public's money is acquitted." There were further Bills on juvenile offenders, factory reform and relief of the victims of the Irish potato famine. These were the kind of causes which Leng fought for in Parliament when later he became M.P. for Dundee.

On the home front, he kept a constant and critical eye on the town council. Alexander Riddoch, who had been Provost of Dundee between 1787 and 1819, had done rather well for himself during his tenure. His acquisitive legacy lived on for many years. But the men in the Town House now knew that they could not return to their old ways, because Leng and his *Advertiser* were ever willing to expose them.

Leng was proud of being known as "Johnny Leng" and one gets the impression that he was well-known about the town as a man of the people.

The business partnership altered in 1852, the year after his arrival. The Limited Liability company of John Leng & Co was formed with Leng as the managing partner. Pattullo and Neish remained as partners.

Leng was seen by the increasing staff as a hands-on employer and a man who took a great interest in their welfare. Looking back in 1901, he said :

*"For many years, I knew every man and boy, and latterly every girl and young woman in the place. It was my custom, after I had finished my editorial work to go upstairs into the caseroom (*where type was set and pages made up) *and stand by the upmaker as he composed both the advertisement and editorial pages of the paper. I regarded upmaking as a work of art, deserving personal superintendence. When that was done, I went down to see the first copy printed, sometimes stopping the press until some appalling blunder was corrected."* Some things never change!

In 1859, *The Advertiser* cost threepence ha'penny per copy, and Leng was determined to bring out a daily paper at a ha'penny. This he did with *The Daily Advertiser* which appeared on 4 May of that year. It had four pages measuring 15 by 10 inches and was on the streets at 11am. Sometimes two other editions followed throughout the day. The paper contained extracts from the London dailies and telegrams from the Franco-Prussian war.

It was a huge success, with upwards of 30,000 copies of the first edition being sold. It was an incredible sale, not bad even for the 21st century. Such a circulation was never contemplated and the presses in Argyll Close couldn't cope with this print figure, plus that of a bi-weekly and a weekly. And so the enterprising daily closed on May 23, after 11 issues.

This unsatisfactory situation was faced up to by the acquisition of land on the north side of Bank Street, chosen because of the proximity to Pattullo and Neish's office. The new offices opened on 18 October 1859 and formed the core of the several extensions which followed - more of this in a separate chapter.

The basement of the 1859 building housed the printing machinery, while the publishing office, reporting and editorial rooms were on street level. The caseroom was on the top floor. An office library was established.

The Advertiser was going well. Morale among the staff must have been high and Leng rewarded their efforts in tangible ways. Office outings were organized. The first was held in 1854 and went to Glamis. The second went to St Andrews. Later, horse-drawn coaches went to Dunkeld, Reekie Linn and the Bonnie Hoose o' Airlie. Trains were chartered to take staff to Blair Atholl, Oban and Elie. Steamers took them up to Newburgh and on to the mouth of the Earn. Perhaps Leng got the idea from Coats, the Paisley thread people. They chartered a train and took 6,000 staff to the Trossachs for the day.

In later times, when things were really buzzing and a major new piece of equipment was installed, such as a high-speed press, Leng would hire the Kinnaird Hall in Bank Street and there he would host a slap-up feed, provide entertainment and there would be congratulatory speeches.

The social involvement of staff reached its acme at the time of Leng's Jubilee in 1901 when he chartered "The Fifie" – a Tay ferryboat – had it decked out with bunting and transported 600 guests from Dundee on a lovely summer's afternoon.

Employees, wives, girl friends were received by (the then) Sir John and Lady Leng at their Kinbrae mansion, just up from the ferry terminal, and everyone had the run of the considerable garden. There was a marquee on the lawn, silver-service catering was by one of Sir John's many friends, Mr Lamb of Lamb's Hotel in Reform Street, (later to become the offices of The Alliance Trust).

The band of the Mars training ship played and there was a choir and a conjurer. And then, in the cool of the evening, the guests strolled down to the ferry for their cruise back to Dundee. One cannot think that many Dundee employers would have spent money in thanking their employees in this way. One has just to consider the conditions in the jute factories of the time.

The scene on Kinbrae's lawn at Leng's Jubilee celebrations in 1901

In January 1890, Leng had installed a new press and in celebration, entertained 700 staff and relatives to a "jolly" in the Kinnaird Hall. There was fork-and-knife tea prepared again by A.C. Lamb. The organ played, the *Advertiser* Male Voice Choir sang. Gymnasts cavorted, barbells were exercised and dancing followed. Later, Sir John was presented with his portrait in oils, done by James Archer RSA.

His generosity continued. In honour of his knighthood in 1893, arranged by Gladstone, Leng took his staff on a sail up to Newburgh where they had lunch. They then sailed to Dundee where they had dinner in the Kinnaird Hall, followed by the usual soiree. These liberal acts must have been the talk of a town.

In Leng's early years in Dundee, there were major factors which limited newspaper circulations. These were outwith his control and applied throughout the land. Apart from difficulties with distribution, in the early years of the 19th century, the government imposed a Stamp Duty on newspapers. This was a thinly-veiled method of keeping the working classes in the dark. The idea was to kill off the radical press by pricing them out of the market.

It has to be remembered that the French and American revolutions were recent events and the British government, aware of radical tendencies in this country, priced newspapers out of reach of working people, who were earning less than 10 shillings(50p) per week. In 1815, a newspaper cost 7d(3p) of which 4d(1 1/2p) was tax.

There was also an advertising tax. If you wanted to sell something in 1815, and your advert was 10- 12 lines, you paid the government six shillings (30p). Further, there was a tax on newsprint.

But in 1836, Stamp Duty was reduced to a penny a copy. In 1855, when Leng was really getting into his stride, Stamp Duty - together with the advertising and paper tax - was abolished completely.

Around the same time, roads were being improved, and railways constructed. Towns were being built where copies could be distributed cheaply in the streets. The market expanded hugely.

At one time, a copy was bought and read by perhaps a dozen workers. Now, most people could afford to buy their own.

These financial changes resulted in huge opportunities in publishing. Leng turned his attention to his bi-weekly *Advertiser*, making it a penny daily called *The Dundee Advertiser* on 1 May 1861. In the course of all the changes that had taken place, the paper had sprung from four to ten or twelve pages with seven or eight columns in each.

But now, Leng was looking further afield, firstly at new publications which could be sold nationally, and secondly how national and international news could be brought to his Dundee newspaper offices much more quickly.

*The London office
in Fleet Street.*

CHAPTER 4

THE SCOPE WIDENS

FROM the earliest days of *The Advertiser*, having London representation was seen as important. In 1802, the second editor and then proprietor, James Saunders, appointed a London agent to sell the paper and also advertising space. But there was no editorial input to Dundee from the south then.

When the *Advertiser* was a bi-weekly, it featured mainly local affairs, and so news was easily gathered. But when it became a daily in 1861, it majored on national events and politics, and this information had to be acquired regularly and reliably.

When Leng had arrived in Dundee in 1851, the Post Office was in the east corner of the Town House (now demolished, but on the site of the City Square). In charge was Mr Bell the postmaster, and three or four assistants. There was no telegram or telephone office. It was some years before a telegraph wire connected Dundee with Edinburgh and the south. Dundee telegrams were either posted or sent by train to and from Edinburgh.

Around 1854, a wire was installed in the Customs House and Leng's appprentices waited there to rush important messages up to the printing offices in Argyll Close.

In June 1870, Leng completed arrangements with the Post office for a direct, private wire link between Dundee and London. An office for the Wire Room was established at 145 Fleet Street. It operated between 6pm and 6 am and was reserved for items like the stock market closing prices, and any urgent matters which related directly to Dundee businessmen. These would be in the second edition of *The Advertiser* next morning. Dundee money was being invested all over the world and up-to date financial intelligence was a circulation builder.

This special wire link was in addition to the normal public wire which delivered hundreds of messages from all over the world to the GPO in Dundee and thence to the Bank Street offices. The GPO then was on the site of the present Thomson Meadowside office.

As an aside, a pneumatic tube existed in modern times between the Meadowside and *Advertiser* offices, being buried under The Howff. There were frequent blockages and the engineering staff used great ingenuity to clear the pipe. There were rumours of a passageway also, but I never saw it. It was maybe a bit like the old Dundee story that you could enter the gents' toilet at the top of Hilltown and emerge half a mile away at the at the one at the foot of the hill.

The Howff was the scene of skulduggery between Leng and the rival Thomson firm, who owned *The Courier*. Being first with breaking news was vital and *The Courier* would send someone through the old graveyard at dead of night to listen for *The Advertiser* presses starting up. They would then wait for a time before they started up, thus gaining a possible last-minute scoop.

But back to 1870 and Leng's London Office. This also housed a Special Correspondent who went to the Commons each day and he sent a parliamentary report. This was often quoted as an authoritative source on general as well as Scottish politics. Taken for granted today, this was pretty novel stuff at the time. The early *Advertiser* also included a weekly London Letter, telling of interesting happenings in the capital. It continues today, perhaps the only British paper to carry such a continuous feature.

So important did the London office become, that in 1882 additional premises were taken at 186 Fleet Street.

One of the "no holds barred" bills produced by Leng.

In 1893, the Donside Paper Mill, just west of Aberdeen was taken over by a Limited Liability company with John Leng as chairman. Delivery of sufficient paper when required was no longer a problem and virtually all Leng publications from then on were printed on paper from the north east. Detailed information of Leng's involvement at Donside will be found in a later chapter.

The Advertiser and *The Courier* continued as separate papers and with their own political slants until they came together as one at the end of the 1926 General Strike.

The joint issue had eight pages, five columns per page and each page the same size as the present *Evening Telegraph*. The price was one penny and the paper, titled in gothic script *Dundee Advertiser and The Courier* came out on Monday 17 May 1926.

It has to be remembered that by that time, *The Advertiser* was under the control of D.C. Thomson & Co. A joint arrangement was made in 1905 bringing the Thomson and Leng businesses together. D.C. Thomson & Co still use the name of John Leng & Co for business purposes, and an AGM is held.

CHAPTER 5

THE PEOPLE'S JOURNAL

UPON the abolition of Stamp Duty in 1855, many new newspapers appeared across the land. There were about 105 in Scotland at that time, but not all were successful. Leng remarked "Many of the weeklies were unworthy of the intelligence and character of the respectable portion of the working classes."

His approach to expansion was to take a considered step at a time. In 1855, his whole attention was given to all aspects of his *Advertiser*. He had seen many papers fail and so took time to assess the market.

By 1858 he had done his homework and on Saturday 2 January launched a weekly, in one edition, *The Dundee, Perth and Forfar People's Journal*. It sold 7,000 copies. Prior to the launch he had set up a network of agents to handle the sale. It was priced at one penny and was aimed at the working class, while most newspapers of the time sought out the middle class. A Fife edition was launched on 30 January. An edition for Aberdeenshire, Banff and Kincardine came in 1863, with the arrival of the railway.

The Journal was the first attempt to tell the Scottish country people what was going on in the world outwith their own area. Cities had their daily and bi-weekly papers. Towns had their weeklies which expressed opinions. But in isolated villages, in the countryside and in the glens, were bright, thinking Scots people. News reached them by irregular channels, sometimes by word of mouth, long after events had happened.

So they bought *The Journal* which kept them up to date and they remained steadfastly loyal, the buying habit continuing through successive generations. When Winston Churchill opened the new Leng premises in Fleet Street in 1914, he called *The Journal* – certainly not disparagingly –The Ploughman's Bible. In Forfar, for instance, which could be referred to as a ploughman's town at the time, one out of two houses bought the paper. Nothing appeared in it that could not be read by any member of the family without giving moral offence, a policy commendably continued to this day by D.C. Thomson. One of the aims of the paper was self-improvement.

In April 1858, not long after the launch, Leng told the *Journal* readers that he needed a circulation of 10,000 to make a profit. 5,000 would cover the outlay. By October, the sale was 10,440 but the print figure could not be increased because of limitations of the printing press. That was put right by the completion of the new Bank Street premises and new printing equipment in October 1859.

AUNT KATE'S ALMANAC

COPYRIGHT

FOR 1898.

PRICE ONE PENNY.

PRINCIPAL CONTENTS.

How to Write Love Letters.
Seeking a Situation.
The Home Nurse.
A Crown's worth of Fiction.
The Woman he Marries.
Indoor Games for Children.
Learn Young: Learn Fair.
How to foretell the Weather.
Hallowe'en.
Monthly Work in the Apiary.
Common Accidents.
The Care of Lamps.
What the Hand Tells.
Notable Copies of the Bible.
Emigration.
Health Maxims.
Burgh Holidays.
Weekly Scotch Market Days.
Marketing Table.
Ready Reckoner.
Income and Wages Table.
Gardeners' Remembrancers.
Postal Information.
Church Incomes.
A Proverb for Every Day.
Handy Household Measures.
etc., etc.

Published by the Proprietors of the People's Journal.

One of the many "Aunt Kate" booklets published by The People's Journal.
The character was used virtually until the end of the paper's life.

The readership - and that is normally taken as three times the number of papers actually sold - would therefore be in excess of 30,000. A nice figure to present to advertisers, and therefore a lever to increase revenue.

But that was nothing compared with what was to come. In December 1890, a Dundee accountant certified that he had been over the books and the *Journal* sale for that year had been a total of 5,525,950, an average 212,536 copies per week. Further, sales for the last three months, excluding the Christmas edition, had been 2,854,090, an average of 219,545 for the eight editions then being offered. The paper's best circulation years were between 1890 and 1893, but year-on-year figures did fluctuate. The average weekly sale in 1921 was 187,000. In 1925 233,821 and in 1935, 177,000.

The firm was declaring that one week's issue weighed 17 tons, and it carried more adverts a than any other weekly paper in Scotland. They impressed by stating that if the columns of the paper were pasted end on end, they would reach from Scotland to San Francisco, and that the annual total of columns would reach 60,000 miles further than the distance from the earth to the moon. The paper was sold by 12,000 newsagents.

By that time, there were branches for editorial staff and the receipt of adverts in Aberdeen, Forfar, Arbroath, Montrose, Perth, Cupar, Stirling, Edinburgh and Glasgow.

The interest in reading was accelerated by the Education Acts of 1870 and 1872. Prior to that, there was no great enthusiasm among politicians to educate the masses.

Within 20 years, *The Journal* was the biggest circulation weekly in the UK outside London, and kept that

---

'Advertise, for the life of Business is Printers' Ink."—*C. H. SPURGEON.*

CERTIFICATE OF CIRCULATION

OF THE

PEOPLE'S JOURNAL.

[COPY.]

11 REFORM STREET, DUNDEE,
31st December 1890.

This is to certify that I have this day Examined the Books of the *People's Journal* Newspaper relating to its Circulation, and find that during the Six Months commencing July 5, and ending December 27, 1890, both days inclusive, the Total Number of Copies Printed (exclusive of Christmas Number) was FIVE MILLIONS FIVE HUNDRED AND TWENTY - FIVE THOUSAND NINE HUNDRED AND FIFTY.

5,525,950,

Being a Weekly Average for the Six Months of

212,536 COPIES,

And that for the Three Months Commencing October 4 and ending December 27, 1890, both dates inclusive, the Total Number of Copies Printed (exclusive of Christmas Number) was TWO MILLIONS EIGHT HUNDRED AND FIFTY-FOUR THOUSAND AND NINETY,

2,854,090,

Being a Weekly Average for the Three Months of

219,545 COPIES.

(Signed) DAVID MYLES,
Public Accountant.

THE ABOVE IS THE

IRGEST CERTIFIED CIRCULATION OF ANY SCOTTISH NEWSPAPER
FOR A CONTINUOUS PERIOD.

position until the outbreak of the first world war. Eventually, it ran to 13 editions covering the whole of Scotland and was acknowledged as a national newspaper. England, with a population ten times larger, could only boast one national weekly newspaper.

It had been a success from the start, mainly due to the efforts of its first editor, William D. Latto who was appointed by Leng in 1860. Latto was born in Ceres, Fife, in 1823 and became a handloom weaver. He partly educated himself and gathered enough money to go to a Free Church school. He then became a schoolmaster at Johnshaven in Kincardineshire. He was "a lad of parts" who had a gift for writing in prose and verse which he sent to Leng, who recognized their worth.

Latto remained editor for 38 years, retiring in 1898, during which time his whole energy was devoted to the furtherance of the paper. He knew working class people and was able to aim the content of his paper and its attitudes exactly at them. *The Journal* became their friend. Apart from being editor, he wrote about inspirational Scottish figures from history - William Wallace, Robert the Bruce, Rob Roy, and histories of the clans.

He developed in his readers a pride in Scotland and its achievements. He was supported in this patriotic writing by the prolific and informed George Gilfillan, a liberally-inclined Dundee minister whose name is still remembered today.

Latto wrote about political and social matters in the Doric, under the pen-name of Tammas Bodkin. This style established an even closer rapport with his readers and also sugared the political pill he was putting over to them. In a way, Latto was also showing the worth of the Doric over standard English which was being pushed hard at the time. He said "I think my ain hamely Scotch is every bit as expressive, or even mair sae, than what is ca'd pure English."

His campaigns were not always national ones, but they related to ordinary people. He spoke out against the bothy system where salmon fishermen and farm workers lived in squalid conditions. About men who had been working hard at digging drains for two weeks being dismissed for no reason, about a harmless simpleton in Inchture who was well known and well liked, being locked up in an asylum. By raising matters which affected both town and country people, he drew the two together and – radical as always - promoted solidarity.

During the South African war, the *Journal's* liberal stance caused it to be banned from that part of the empire. Remarkably, the paper got as far as Russia and a reader there sent his copy back to Bank Street with the leader column blacked out by the censor, as proof of what was going on there.

Poor housing in Victorian Scotland came under fire and there was support for an eight-hour working day, and better wages for factory workers. *The Journal* was always looking for, and offering support to, causes which would advance the well-being of its reader, the working man and his family.

At the time, *The Journal* was essentially a supporter of the Liberal Party, although by the turn of the 20th century there was some support for Labour and reports from the conferences of the Scottish Trade Union Congress. The paper spoke out for Home Rule (for Ireland), a watered-down version of which took another century to come to fruition.

At a general election held in the early 1900s, the sitting member for West Perthshire was a South African magnate, supported by wealthy Conservatives. The polling day was fixed – intentionally or otherwise – sufficiently late in the week to allow the Conservative and his supporters to "explain away" *The Journal's* Liberal stance. But Leng had a thunderbolt in store for them. He rushed out a special edition on the eve of the poll. It routed the Conservatives and the Liberal was elected.

Interestingly, two Liberal prime Ministers lived in Leng's immediate circulation area – Henry Campbell Bannerman at Belmont Castle, Meigle and Gladstone's country seat was at Fasque, near Fettercairn.

But the content of the paper wasn't all political, by any means. There were short stories, competitions, poetry, serialised novels. Stories for the children. In 1878 there was a series about "The Families of Forfarshire." The fictional stories were about ordinary people with whom readers could identify – a successful formula still being used in D.C. Thomson magazines a century later.

One serial story was entitled "Bonnie Dundee, or the Enchanted Bullet." On the previous week's announcement there was a romantic picture of Viscount Claverhouse, shown overleaf. The bullet surely refers to the supposed silver one which killed him at Killiecrankie. Again, we have the formula which lends credence to the story, fiction woven around fact. Another serial, suggesting intrigue, was entitled "The Outlawed Heir, or His Secret Wife." Each story always had an alternative title.

Mention should be made of George G. Glass, who was in the editor's chair for 38 years between 1912 and 1950. He was a forceful editor, given to the odd outburst of rage when he would hurl rectangular lumps of lead upon which printing plates were mounted, at the wall. In the writer's time, there were still sharp dents in the plaster opposite the editor's chair. He died in 1958, leaving £13,200 which was a reasonable sum in these days.

His daughter, Barbara, was the editor of the Thomson women's weekly, *Family Star*. She inherited her father's temperament, and ran a very tight ship. But underneath it all, she had a heart of gold and any young journalist who trained under her would get a job anywhere. From the early days, Leng's policy was to employ women journalists, where their

specialised talents would further the appeal of his papers. He said that they were able to "edit, sub-edit, and report. There are appropriate openings for well- educated and clever girls. It adds grace and charm to the literary staff and sweetens relationships of the whole establishment." (I can say with full knowledge that this policy was pursued by D.C.T., much to their credit. Regardless of sex, talent was always recognized.)

When the writer worked on *The Journal* in the 1950s, the editor was Jimmy Hood, an ex-Scots Guardsman, pillar of the Kirk and strongly anti-drink. He had fallen heir to a long temperance tradition. I have seen a letter from 1935 written by the Bank Street manager, G.T. Watson. It was to a member of the Aberdeen office staff who was organizing the firm's stand at the Royal Highland Show. Watson wrote "We do not think it is a good plan to have anything of the nature of refreshments on the stand. It simply attracts undesirables." Wonderful stuff!

In this context, Leng himself is quoted as saying - *"I attribute much of my success to a capacity for hard and long, sustained work, despite lack of physical robustness. Such health as was given to me was carefully preserved by avoiding every excess. I have always worked by water power. Too many men of fine natural organization have I seen incapacitate themselves for efforts when required by indulging their appetites. Temperance in all things should be carefully studied."*

In the 1950s there were still editions covering virtually every country area in Scotland. But the paper had changed greatly from its earlier format. It had to, for the world had changed. Country people had cars, telephones, televisions and a wide choice of reading material to keep themselves informed. The war was over, and *The Journal* was no longer being sent in large numbers to soldiers overseas.

In 1866, there were five editions – Dundee, Fife, Forfar, Perth, Aberdeen and South. In 1909 there were editions for Perth city and Perthshire, Forfar and Forfarshire, Clackmannan, Aberdeen, Glasgow, Banff, Edinburgh, Fife, Argyll and the Isles, North of England, Ireland and Dundee. It dropped to nine editions during World War 2 and remained at that number until 1969. By 1976 only Inverness, Aberdeen, Argyll and Dundee were left.

Social change is one of the reasons that some newspapers die. They outlive their usefulness and so it was with *The People's Journal*. Gradually, the number of editions diminished until only the Dundee one was left. The grand old lady was laid to rest in 1990 in Bank Street where she was born 132 years before.

CHAPTER 6

THE PEOPLE'S FRIEND

A S we have seen, Leng encouraged his readers to send in stories and articles for publication. Columns of good quality amateur material were published over the decades in *The People's Journal*. Some of these "finds" became prolific professionals. Leng was almost certainly the first editor to mine this source of material, particularly fiction.

Apart from filling the paper in an interesting way, it is a proven circulation builder because it allows the contributor, who is also a reader, to feel he is a worthwhile part of the paper. D.C. Thomson's *Sunday Post* built its enormous circulation largely on reader participation.

Part of a letter from John Leng to David Pae which resulted in Pae becoming editor of The Friend.

This "invite" to readers was so successful that *The Journal* had nothing like enough space to take all the material which Leng felt just had to be used. And so, to absorb it, he launched "*The People's Friend*" on Wednesday (to keep it away from *The Journal* sale day) 13 January 1869. Winter has always been a good time to start a new paper, with the long dark nights.

The literary staff of *Chambers Journal* had moved south to London in 1859, leaving a gap in the market to be filled by a new popular Scottish magazine. There was a big demand for Scottish material and several people tried to fill the gap. Most were local attempts, and failed.

Leng knew what to do, and the standards of *The Friend*, based on Scottish life, were purposely aimed at people who lived in the cities. At a time when education was highly valued by the masses and rightly seen

THE PEOPLE'S FRIEND

A Monthly Miscellany in connection with the "People's Journal."

No. 1. {REGISTERED FOR TRANSMISSION ABROAD.} WEDNESDAY, JANUARY 13, 1869. PRICE ONE PENNY.

THE STORY TELLER.

FAITHFUL AND TRUE—A SAD STORY FOR THE HAPPY CHRISTMAS TIME.

BY GLAUCUS.

"A sad tale's best for winter"—*Shakspeare.*

CHAPTER I.

There was a large party at dinner the day I arrived at Dolremmet Castle. Next day was the 12th of August, and the Earl of A—— had all his old friends about him, who for years had shot the grouse on his moors. The dinner party was like any other dinner party at a country house—perhaps a little merrier and less formal than most ones, as almost every one of the guests had already known each other well. The Countess was not yet an old woman, and did her duty of hostess very gracefully, as she formed the centre of a lively circle at the top of the table, while the Earl, a fine, hearty, middle-aged man, performed the duties of host as no one save an English gentleman knows how. Lady Fanny, the eldest daughter, whom I had the pleasure of taking into dinner, was a very old and firm friend of mine. Without being striking handsome, she was always considered good-looking. A clear, brilliant complexion, lots of dark hair, pearly teeth, a good figure, and a faculty for dressing well, were her chief characteristics, while a power of pleasant talk, combined with a keen appreciation of humour, rendered her a very agreeable companion. Opposite me sat Lady Edith, the most perfect representative of quiet English beauty. And yet, though her beauty was entirely English, in some respects it was difficult to describe. None of her features, except her eyes, were altogether perfect in themselves, but taken together they formed an exquisite harmony and delicacy of proportion. Looking across to her, and seeing her face dimpling into smiles, and her clear beautiful complexion changing its colour every moment, I think I never saw anything so fascinating. Her eyes were remarkably beautiful. The moment you looked into her face you were irresistibly drawn to her eyes, and they so fascinated you that you would gaze all the time she was talking to you into depths of quiet blue. They had all the silent beauty of those of a dumb animal, while at the same time they teemed with meaning, and were radiant with expression. On her right hand sat a young artist of great promise, who was employing his spare time at the Castle in painting a likeness of Helen for the Countess, and who, to judge from his manner to her, was aided in his task not a little by a third party, who added not a little to the truth and beauty of the picture he painted. The only other person whom it is necessary for our story to recal at the table was the Hon. Augustus Weir, a nephew of the Earl's, and, as he had no sons of his own, the heir to his estates. It was generally understood that with her father's and mother's approval he was a suitor for Edith's hand, and on this particular occasion did not seem much to relish the attentions which the young artist lavished upon her, or the fond way in which she seemed to return them. After the ladies had retired, Rosetti—for so the artist was named—came over to my side of the table, wishing to strike up a friendship, as he had been a friend of my brother's in Rome, three years before. We soon got into a long and interesting talk about Rome, and the people we knew there; and my friend was describing with a true artist's ardour a new statue that had been discovered some short time before he left, when we were interrupted by Weir crying out from the other side of the table, loud enough for every one to hear—"When you fellows are done talking shop, I wish you would pass the wine." Rosetti immediately fired up, and had I not laid my hand on his arm and whispered a word in his ear, would have replied with some bitter sarcasm to the impudent remark. As it was, he passed the wine in silence, and Weir, though he had been drinking pretty freely, seeing he had gone a little too far, continued, "Well, the wine had been before you for at least ten minutes, and I thought you would never be done talking about that piece of cut stone," and, emptying his glass of port, continued, "For my part I can't see anything in these stone Venuses you rave about—healthy flesh and blood beauty for me." A reply was interrupted by the Earl crying out, "Well, Rosetti, have you yet found the proper shade of blue for fair Edith's eyes?" The shade of anger died away from the artist's face, and, smilingly, he replied, "Oh, sir, that would be impossible, but we have managed a little better to-day. Lady Edith was kind enough to put her whole afternoon at my disposal. She is so patient with me."

"A precious sight too much, Ed.," I heard Weir mutter between his teeth.

"Then," said the Earl, "we will join the ladies, and after tea we will go and have a peep at the picture."

We did so, and in about an hour afterwards found ourselves in the studio. As Rosetti drew aside the curtain before the picture, an exclamation of delight and surprise broke from the lips of every one present. As he arranged the lights so as to bring it out to advantage, the first impression of all of us was the life-likeness. After some little examination of it, what struck me most about the painting was not so much the evident genius which it displayed—although that was undoubtedly great—but the fond care with which the artist appeared to have lingered on every line and curve of expression, as if the brush had been reluctant to leave any one part of the picture, but fain would have lingered for ever on each. Every one was enchanted. Some congratulated Lady Edith, others the artist, and others the Earl, who stood silently gazing at the picture, but at last turning round to his daughter, he kissed her long and fondly, saying, "I never knew till now that my own darling Nelly was so lovely," and then, looking to the artist, "My dear Rosetti, we all owe you a debt of gratitude." Weir was the only one who had no complimentary word to say either to the painter or his subject. He had not yet quite recovered from the wine after dinner, and the mixture of jealousy and heated blood in his face was a sight not pleasant to see. On returning to the drawing-room, I had a long confidential talk with Lady Fanny about the evident *affaire de cœur* between her sister and the artist, and neither of us were able to forbode anything save sorrow and pain from the circumstance.

In pleasant enjoyment—shooting, fishing, riding, driving, playing croquet and Aunt Sally on the lawn, or, if the day was wet, knocking about the billiard balls—the days passed rapidly away. As the day for Rosetti's departure drew near, it was painful to see the two—Lady Helen and he—they were constantly together; and if in the crowded room they could not talk as they wished, the longing, wistful looks they exchanged were sad, and apparent to every one but the Earl and Countess, who evidently never dreamt of such a thing, or anything but friendliness between the two. Then the picture was constantly requiring some finishing touches, and in my room I could hear them conversing together in low tones, and sometimes I thought I heard a sob from the Lady Edith, as if some great sorrow was welling up in her heart. Saturday morning, the day on which he had to be up in town, came. We were assembled in the breakfast room, waiting for the Earl to come down and read prayers, when a message came desiring Sir John W—— to do so, as the Earl was engaged. Lady Edith, who was sitting next me, gave a great start. For a moment a deadly pallor came over her sweet face, and in the next it was suffused with a painful crimson. This was, however, unnoticed, and prayers were proceeded with. The Earl was in his usual place at breakfast, and made excuses for Rosetti, who, he said, was too busy making preparations for his departure to join us just yet. After the morning meal was over, I repaired to my bed-room to arrange some fishing tackle, and as I did so I heard a hurried passing to and fro in the studio. In a little I heard a rustle of silk and a timid knock at the door. It was immediately opened, and through my half-open door I could see Lady Edith enter. My tackle was either dreadfully entangled that day, or my mind was wandering on some other topic, for I took a long time to arrange it. Just as I was going out, I heard a great sob, and Rosetti exclaim—"Well, darling, I shall be faithful and true till death, and do you remember the Post Office of C——. In a second or two the door opened, and Rosetti hurried out, looking pale and haggard. As I knew Lady Edith could not be long in following, I half closed my door and waited. In a little she did come, walking listlessly, with her little head bowed on her bosom, which was heaving with "wild unrest," and her dove eyes were red with tears. I waited till she was fairly out of sight, and then, as I was going out, I thought I heard an exclamation of smothered rage from the studio. I looked in, but seeing no one, supposed it was mere delusion on my part. While I was waiting in the stable-yard for the rest of the fishing party, Weir came down and called out for his groom. His face had a strange mixture of rage, jealousy, hate, and triumph in it. I asked him if he was not going to join our party as he had intended, and he replied, 'No;' that he had to go to a neighbouring town on some business. After we returned from our fishing excursion Fanny told me what I had already conjectured had happened. Rosetti had told the Earl of his love for Edith. The Earl told him in return that, however much he might have esteemed him as a friend and admired him as a genius, it would not be becoming to have him as a son-in-law, and that he had already promised his daughter Edith to Mr Weir.

Poor Lady Edith! from that day she was never her former bright and happy self. Sometimes at lunch she used to be a little like the old Edith, but in the afternoon, after her ride, which I noticed always took the direction of C——, she was always sad and despondent. The only pleasure she seemed to have was in caressing her fine St Bernard dog, Roma, which Rosetti had given her before leaving. The end of my stay at Dolremmet Castle had now come, and I could not help drawing a contrast between what it was when I first arrived and when I left, for Lady Edith's evident suffering was acutely felt by all in the house. In driving to the town, where I got my train, I had to pass through the village of C——. As I passed through, a thought suddenly struck me, and I bid the man drive to the Post Office, and found the rural postmaster, a civil, simple countryman, and inquired at him, in a casual way, if there were any letters for Lady Edith. He replied, "No, sir; I wish there were. The poor lady comes here day after day, and it makes my heart sore to say 'No!' to her. She takes on so, and turns away quickly to hide her face." As he said this, a door opened, and a woman, with an ugly, wicked face, asked what I had to do with Lady Edith's letters?—if there were any for her she would give them to her herself. I didn't reply, but, thanking the man for his civility, went away with a strange feeling of dissatisfaction and distrust at the woman's looks.

Christmas, dear old merry Christmas, with its gaieties and happy family meetings—above all, with its hallowed memories—found me once more at my old quarters in the Castle. There were a good many visitors besides myself—Mr Weir amongst the number. I was greatly shocked and grieved to see how ill poor Lady Edith was looking. The colour had quite died out of her face, and her features seemed pinched and wan. I heard from her sister that another trouble was weighing upon her. Mr Weir had again begun his attentions to her, and the Earl had been pressing her to fix an early month for her marriage with him. She put her father off from week to week, pleading ill health, but she was beginning to see that this would not always do. In her sorrow she seemed like some poor little flower, which, rudely shaken with wind and rain

The cover of the first People's Friend.

as a way out of poverty, *The Friend* encouraged literacy and self improvement although the pill was well sweetened.

The first issue had 16 pages of closely-packed type and no illustrations to break it up. Indeed, illustrations didn't come into publications generally until 20 years later and Leng was the first proprietor outside London to introduce them. The only drawings of any kind were advertisements on the back and front covers, inside and out.

Leng himself wrote to his new readership about the aims and objects of his new baby.

"And now as to what we intend to do….. we intend that fully one half of *The Friend* shall be devoted to fiction…… The paper being intended for fireside reading, nothing will be admitted into its columns having the slightest tendency to corrupt the morals of either old or young. We shall aim at as much variety as possible, and we shall always keep in view the blending of instruction with amusement."

With *The Friend*, as with *The Journal*, John Leng consciously created a pride in all aspects of Scottish life – characters, attitudes, humour, religion, language. It was never intended to be fine literature. Leng created in Dundee an organisation to meet these needs and all his employees believed implicitly in what they were doing. This says much for his own sense of editorial direction and leadership.

The serial stories were invariably set in Scotland and even in the writer's time the editor and the person who was going to write the story would go to the place where it would be set, and stay for several days to get the flavour of it. Local characters would be woven into the story to lend authenticity.

The Friend was a natural medium for spin-off "specials" and over the years, things like *The Friend Cook Book* have been wonderful money-spinners. *The Scottish Cookery Book* was published in 1877. Its sales pitch read " Guid plain rules for makin' guid plain meats, suitable for sma' purses, big families and Scotch stomachs." Not quite the slick copy-writing of today but within a few months it had sold 25,000 copies. The twelfth edition sold 35,000. It was even pirated in New York.

Booklets were published on social etiquette, letter writing, sewing, household tips, children's games, puzzles and many more. These "Specials" went out under the name of other titles too. In 1915, the 4th Black Watch took terrific casualties at the Battle of Loos. It was Dundee's Flodden, for the battalion had been largely raised in the town. Hardly a home was not affected in some way. Leng produced *The Dinna Forget Book*, a tasteful *Advertiser* souvenir dedicated to the fallen.

The Friend took every opportunity to get itself involved with its readership. Slides showing

Scottish or Lakeland scenes were prepared, and lent to various societies for winter shows. Readers were invited to contribute to good causes – funds raised provided three cots for children at Dundee Royal Infirmary.

Much of the paper was given over to self-improvement – children's flower competitions, the study of botany, Civil Service exam papers (!) The editorial formula certainly worked, as evidenced by *The Friend* topping the reading list at the Mitchell Library in Glasgow.

Dress patterns were introduced in 1896 and this department expanded greatly, employing many skilled women. It was big business. It survived until the 1970s when prices in the big stores made it uneconomic to make clothes at home, and further, working women had less time.

Another reason for the magazine's success was that the writers had the common touch and knew what the readers wanted. John Leng had the uncanny knack of recognizing latent editorial talent in amateurs and turning them into part of a professional team with a common purpose. In the writer's experience, which included managing the women's and teenage magazine department in D.C. Thomson, *Friend* editors were really devoted to the job and steered the magazine along with a fine and unerring touch. The editor of *The Friend* was certainly "somebody" in the organization and I'm sure, still is. Editorial policy was seldom, if ever, queried.

The Friend is essentially a fiction-based magazine, but a leavening of cooking, travel, nature and fashion features have been incorporated over the decades. Change has always been subtle and gradual. The result is that the magazine remains successful with a loyal readership which is the envy of many other publishers. It is the oldest women's magazine in the English-speaking world.

CHAPTER 7

ANNIE S. SWAN

O F all the amateur fiction writers "discovered" by Leng, the most successful by a long way was Annie S. Swan. Through the serial stories published in *The Friend* and the books she wrote, she developed a world-wide following and was a national figure in Britain, even being presented at the court of Queen Victoria. Prime Minister Gladstone was a follower.

She won a Leng Christmas story competition at the age of 18, and never looked back. Her first story of any length was written in 1882. Her *Friend* stories tended to be light reading but under her married name of Mrs Burnett-Smith her books encompassed social issues of the time. She stood as a Liberal candidate at one point.

Part of her upbringing was in Kinghorn and there she met her future husband, a teacher at Star, Markinch. He became a medical doctor. During the first world war, she made two trips to America to rally support for Britain and to encourage them to increase food supplies. She also made visits to the troops on the Western Front, and raised money for the Hut Fund – wooden huts just behind the front line which provided comforts for the troops.

After the war, she and her husband bought the estate of Bandrum, near Dunfermline. After his death, she settled at Gullane and died there in 1943, leaving £27,000. This was a lot of money at the time, and must put her near the top of the earnings tree of Leng/Thomson fiction writers.

These non-staff people were paid per thousand words and the rate was generally low and not increased very often, and involuntarily. Swan would be regarded by the firm as a special case, just as Dudley D. Watkins was by D.C. Thomson at a later period.

The Dundee GPO where Leng's cables arrived. The building was demolished to make way for the Thomson offices, opened in 1906.

CHAPTER 8

THE EVENING TELEGRAPH

BY 1877, Leng's publishing empire was well-established and he did the obvious thing – by producing another newspaper. *The Evening Telegraph* launched on 13 March of that year, in two editions and under the editorship of William Fisher. The price was one halfpenny. In the Leng tradition, it was radical and reforming.

There was the latest news which arrived in Dundee via telegraph, "The Cream of the London and Scottish Press, Freshest Local and District Intelligence". Also included were athletic and sporting news, literary extracts and a ladies column by a lady editor.

The early years weren't all moonlight and roses. Leng said "In some respects, this was my pet child. It was weak and sickly and nearly killed me in nursing and tending it. But now is thriving and vigorous." A single edition of the *Tele* would represent a whole year's circulation of *The Advertiser* in 1860. Eventually, *The Evening Telegraph* claimed the largest circulation of any ha'penny daily paper outside Glasgow or Edinburgh. You could subscribe to it for 26 shillings a year(approx £1.25).

As ever, many circulation boosters were tried. Trophies were offered to local sports clubs and a magnificent cup was put up for the Scottish Amateur Golf Championship. This was ignored by the elite clubs but raised the standard of the artisan game, particularly at Carnoustie.

The earliest circulation figure available for the paper is for May 1899 when it was selling 21,420. On 22 January 1900, the rival Thomson organisation brought out their *Evening Post* but unfortunately, no circulation figures for its early days can be found. However, the two papers amalgamated on 17 May 1905, which would be about the time that Thomsons took a controlling interest in the Leng business. In their usual canny way, DCT may have decided correctly that Dundee could not support two evening papers. At that time, the combined sale of the two papers was 46,913.

The *"Tully"* as it is affectionately known in Dundee appeared in seven editions at one point and after the relaxation of newsprint controls after the second world war, sales soared to what is almost certainly their highest point, a remarkable 77,453 per day in February 1951. Television's early evening local and national news were just a few years away.

Eventually, the paper was published in four editions, until 2007. The 5th came out just after mid-day, the 6th and City editions followed throughout the afternoon and the Late Extra was on the streets to catch workers going home. In 2009, there are three editions – the 1st, the County and the Late Extra.

The *"Tully"* is still doing well under its original Leng masthead and, against the trend of other Scottish evening papers, is showing an increase at the time of writing.

Delivery boys "in uniform" loading The Evening Telegraph in Bank Street. Probably the 1920s.

A drawing of the long premises in their final form, drawn by David Small, an artist with the firm.

CHAPTER 9

THE DEVELOPMENT OF BANK STREET

WHEN Leng arrived in Dundee in 1851 the *Advertiser* office was in the Argyll Close, off the Overgate. He knew right away that larger premises would be required. A site became available in Bank Street, conveniently near the offices of Pattullo and Neish, Leng's partners. The first portion of the building which would eventually take up almost the whole of the north side of the street was opened in October 1859. The frontage was 60 feet.

It consisted of a basement and two storeys above street level. The publishing, editorial and reporting rooms were on ground level, the type was composed on the upper level and the printing was done in the basement (because of the weight of the press).

When *The Advertiser* became a daily in 1861, the pressure on space became extreme and the building was extended westward, doubling its size. *The People's Friend*, which started as a monthly in 1869 went weekly the following year and so a complete storey had to be added above in 1870.

Two years later, the builders were back for the fourth time. A five storey extension, with basement and a 62 feet frontage was added westwards. This gave increased space for the literary staff, plus a jobbing department, where printing for outside firms was carried out. This brought in good money from reliable payers like Burgh Councils. Voters' Rolls for Forfarshire, Rolls of Eminent Burgesses, Annual Valuation Rolls and the massive tome showing buildings of old Dundee – and now very collectable – *Lamb's Dundee*. Colour printing was introduced in 1884.

In 1890, another extension was completed, and also a tunnel under Bank Street which led to a storage area on the south side for reels of printing paper.

The final addition to the north side of the street, completed in 1899, was an architectural feat. The roof of the whole building was removed, a storey added, and a new roof put on without losing an hour of production. In 1859, the square footage of the new office was 5472. In 1900, it was 40,350.

As each extension was completed, the latest machinery to improve production was incorporated. Leng was always at the forefront of technology. One of the greatest advances was the introduction of Linotype machines, which did away with hand- setting of type. A man and a Linotype machine could set 7,000 letters per hour, four times faster than hand-setting. These machines were used in the industry until the introduction of photo-setting in the 1960s.

One difficulty which was not easy to overcome was coverage of events which were some distance from a telephone. So, in 1889, Leng installed a large number of homing pigeons in a loft in Bank Street. These were taken in baskets to places like Barry/Buddon army camp and Forthill cricket ground. Experimentally, birds were taken to Montrose, Perth and Carlisle and came home in remarkably quick time, with short reports on rice paper attached to their legs.

There is a story that Dundee F.C's manager was given a pigeon to take to Parkhead for a needle match with Celtic. Dundee won 2-1 and the manager, in a state of high excitement, opened the basket and said to the pigeon " Celtic one, Dundee two, awa ye go and tell them".

Meanwhile virtually all of the south side was being acquired piecemeal, and its development was of this nature. When I went to work there on the fiction department of *The People's Journal* in 1954, it was warren of pokey offices lit by solitary electric light bulbs usually minus shades, back stairs and passage ways. I was always surprised that skeletons were not found of unfortunate sub editors who had failed to make it back to the street.

The Scots Magazine was there, as was the Photo Lab and the Subscribers department, and a large department which produced thousands of paper dress patterns to send all over the UK – a money spinner started by John Leng. All of this conglomeration went south to the Overgate, and the odd back door offered a quiet escape route for operatives who wanted to be away sharp to be on the first tee at Carnoustie.

Incidentally, message boys on bikes had no need of GPS systems to navigate between Bank Street and Meadowside and the East Station in Dock Street. Evening papers for Broughty Ferry and all points east were conducted at breakneck speed through a myriad of pends to catch the train. Some afficionados could judge things finely, hurtling up the ramp at the end of the platform and throwing the rolled-up papers through the open window of the guard's van as the train pulled out.

With advancing technology, a new pressroom had to be built. This was more or less on what is now the access area of the Overgate car park. Printing of *The Courier* and *The People's Journal* moved to this pressroom with its giant Headliner press in April 1974. Like everything else in Bank Street, it was built to last. When the demolition men came along eventually they thought they would never get through the foundations for the Headliner press. Printing of *The Evening Telegraph* moved from Meadowside to the Headliner pressroom in May 1983.

In June 1991, all Dundee newspaper production moved from Bank Street to state-of-the-art and purpose-built premises at East Kingsway. In January 1992, the newspaper editorial and other departments also moved to Kingsway. Bank Street was sold off, the south side becoming the Overgate car park and the noble north side a tasteful conversion to ground floor business premises, with flats above.

Fortunately, the developers retained even the names of the old publications on the outside of the buildings and the fine original detail of the building itself can be seen from the upper floors of the car park.

CHAPTER 10

THE DONSIDE PAPER MILLS

PAPER of a sort had been made at Gordon's Mills on the lower reaches of the River Don, just west of Aberdeen, since 1696. Over the years, the buildings expanded and in 1888, a brave new company was formed, with a capital of £50,000.

Because of recession, foreign competition and poor prices, it went bust three years later.

Enter Sir John Leng and Mr James Pattullo in June 1893. They bought the mill and machinery from the Liquidator for £11,000. Not a bad bit of business. Less than a month later, the Donside Paper Company was formed. It was private limited company with seven equal shareholders, none of whom came from Aberdeen.

One of the first objects of the new company was to buy the leasehold property known as Gordon's Mills from Sir John Leng and James Pattullo. The authorized capital of the company was £25,000 in 5000 shares of £5, of which £16,000 was issued initially. The registered office was 1 Bank Street, Dundee – the business premises of lawyer James Pattullo. John Leng was the first chairman.

The other shareholders were –
James Pattullo, solicitor, Blairgowrie.
William C. Leng, newspaper proprietor, Dundee (Sir John's son).
Charles M. Pattullo, papermaker, Dundee.
Catherine Westwood, spinster, Cupar, Fife.
Alex Banks, printing manager, Dundee.
William Low, advertising manager, Dundee.
Henry A. Pattullo, solicitor, Dundee (also company secretary).

Charles Pattullo managed the mill for £5 per week. He also got a bonus geared to the percentage by which the declared dividend exceeded 5%. Performance related pay is nothing new.

The company operated one machine, producing mainly paper on reels, which were suitable for the Leng presses in Dundee. This reduced costs and wastage. Weekly output was 50 tons.

With a narrow product range the first year gave a profit of £2,267, a handsome return on capital. Wages paid were £1,945 and salaries £408.

I don't know when the Leng financial interest in the mill ended, but in 1911, Donside turned itself into a public company. I do know that when DCT had trouble with the print unions in 1953, a lot of the paper which helped keep their publications going came from Aberdeenshire. And even in the 1980s D.C. Thomson remained faithful customers of Donside. Sometimes they paid upfront, which was appreciated by the troubled mill.

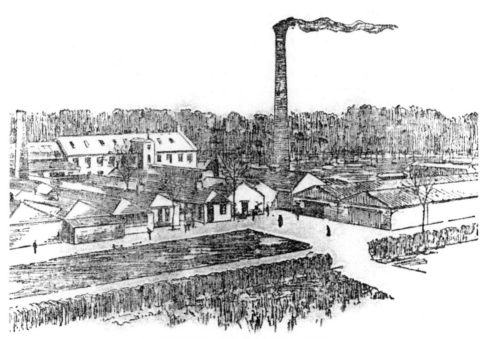

DONSIDE PAPER WORKS

*One of the many supplements put out by Leng and which
caught the public's mood. This one was issued after the
battle of Loos in 1915 when The 4th Black Watch,
largely recruited in Dundee, was decimated.*

CHAPTER 11

LENG'S PRACTICAL CONTRIBUTIONS TO DUNDEE

L ENG found time to take part in civic affairs, the improvement of the city and the good of the people. He pioneered many schemes through the pen and the spoken word. One of the largest was the City Improvement Act in the late 1870s, which renovated the town and eased developments in trade. He was an original mover and shaker.

He fought for a new infirmary to be built near Barrack Park. The original infirmary on the south side of Bucklemaker Wynd (now Victoria Road) was started by two people, one of whom was Dr Stewart who also began *The Advertiser*. A new Royal Infirmary opposite Barrack Park was opened 1855.

*

The Corn Exchange was established in 1856 by Leng's friend, Sir John Ogilvy. Ogilvy offered land on the south side of Bank Street which he and others had bought. Although it was meant also to be used by the public for concerts, classes, meetings and a public saleroom, it was not fully utilized. Leng was prominent in a company formed to acquire the building and adapt it. It was administered by a committee which included John Leng and Lord Kinnaird and was opened in 1858 as the Kinnaird Hall. The building eventually became the Kinnaird cinema.

The building stood on the south side of Bank Street, some thirty yards in from Reform Street. After The Kinnaird cinema, as it became, it was demolished, the vacant site was used for access, partly to Leng premises and partly to what was the Bank of Scotland which fronted on to Reform Street, and which is now a rather grand-looking pub.

*

Leng helped form The Eastern Club where Dundee businessmen lunched and put the world to rights. He also helped found the Technical College, now the University of Abertay Dundee.

*

Baxter Park was donated to Dundee by Sir David Baxter and his two sisters. Leng had a blunt hand in that. He told Sir David that his father, William Baxter hadn't done much for Dundee and asked what he was going to do about it.

*

He strongly advocated acquiring Balgay Park for the recreation of the people of Dundee, which happened in 1871. For similar reasons he advocated acquiring the Law.

*

The British Association for the Advancement of Science came to Dundee in 1867, and Leng became the local secretary and convener of the exhibition committee. It was said to be one of the most successful ever held.

*

The Old Steeple was renovated in 1870-72. Leng donated six new bells and others were recast. This augmented the number of bells to eight.

*

The Lintrathen water supply placed Dundee in an enviable position in Britain. Monikie reservoir, opened in 1846 was soon insufficient and in 1870 a scheme introduced to build Lintrathen. The man who designed it installed the pipes on the wrong route, as Leng had told him he had, but eventually it was successfully re-routed.

*

The site for the Albert Institute was to be feud out for smaller buildings but Leng said it should be reserved for a large civic building. In this he was successful. The Town Council took control in 1867 and built a free library and art gallery known as the Albert Institute. Leng had also been a promoter of free libraries.

He did much to organize Miss Baxter's gift to found University College and got government grants for it. He was a governor before his entitlement to be so as an MP.

*

He had been a student of James Bowman Lindsay who wrote an article in *The Advertiser* in 1834, saying he had succeeded in making electric light. Leng described it as the light of the future and wrote a pamphlet on it.

*

He promoted the removal of slums under the Improvement Act, the extension of the harbour and the formation of what we now know as The Esplanade. The proof of the latter is show in a sketch which appeared in *The Advertiser* as one of Leng's early attempts to introduce illustrations. He was the first publisher outside London to adopt the techniques.

*

He wrote about the transfer of water and gas supplies from private companies to the corporation and the municipalisation of the tramways.

CASKET PRESENTED TO SIR JOHN LENG BY HIS STAFF ON THE OCCASION OF HIS JUBILEE, 1901.

He fought for Dudhope Castle not to be demolished and for tenements not to be built in Barrack Park.

*

Soon after his arrival in Dundee, he bought shares in the Dundee Perth and London Shipping Company, became its Chairman, and by his far-seeing improvements contributed to the development of the firm.

*

He was also a member of the Chamber of Commerce and delivered addresses on various occasions.

*

He was involved with the foundation and progress of what is now The Alliance Trust. He was also one of the original Dundee Board of The Mortgage Co and it was at the request of the other members that, in 1876, he made his first trip to America to visit some of the places where investments had been made, accompanied by the Earl of Airlie.

*

Among the articles Leng wrote are Some European Cities and Rivers (1897), Electric Light by Gas Companies (1878), Scottish Banking Reform(1881), Practical Politics (1885), Dealings with the Unemployed (1886), Home Rule All Round (1890), Excessive Patent Fees(1891), Nationalization - the Dream of the Labour Party (1895).

*

There was also The Utopia of Plato, The Progress of Printing, Composing and Rotary Printing Machines, Two Literary Premiers - Beaconsfield and Gladstone,

Sir John Leng. M.P.

CHAPTER 12

THE MEMBER FOR DUNDEE 1889 - 1905

L ENG was offered the Liberal candidicy for east Fife in 1885 but refused it. In the 1886 General Election, 16 invitations came from various constituencies but he declined to be considered.

But in 1889, the Dundee MP, J.F.B. Firth died and Leng was adopted as the Liberal candidate and was returned unopposed. This is what he said in his adoption speech -

"My memory carries me back through 60 years to a time very different from this, when the conditions of life for the masses of the people were far more severe; when the hours of labour were long and uncontrolled; when women and children were kept in mills and factories 14, 15, and 16 hours out of the 24.

"When miners slaved underground and many worked above ground, until flesh and bone were exhausted; when everything was heavily taxed, when the Corn Laws enriched the landlords and impoverished the people; when not only bread, the meat, the butter, the tea, the sugar, the salt , the pepper, the candles – everything in daily use - was exorbitantly priced by a system of taxation foolishly – if not fiendishly - devised to mulct the necessities and diminish the comforts of the industrious poor.

"I am old enough to remember these bitter times of privation, bordering on actual famine, against which bread riots, the burning of stacks, and the Chartist agitation were natural protests. In my boyhood, I was so close to a witness to the sufferings of the poor…it led me to a resolve not to lead an idle and useless life, but to try to raise the condition of the people.

"It was the saying of a man of great genius 'Forget not the dream of thy youth'. My ideal might have been a dream, but I have not forgotten it.

"A world where men are no longer valued by their accumulated wealth, in which there was no hereditary privilege and no class distinction, but all men had equal rights and opportunities. Where temperance had dismissed the policeman, and closed the prisons and workhouses, in which the benefits of machinery and science led to a general curtailment of the hours of labour. In which more abundant leisure was accompanied by intellectual and moral elevation….

"This might have been a dream, but it is a dream for which I have lived, and still live. If every man did the little that he was able to do, much would be achieved." He entered parliament in September 1889 and was knighted in 1893 at Osbourne House in the Isle of Wight, and went on to hold the Dundee seat with large majorities until 1905.

In Parliament, he spoke for a myriad of issues over a long period. The strand which ran through most of his campaigns was for social improvement and equality.

Things like payments to be made to injured seamen, the excessive hours of railway employees, improvement of conditions of military and naval personnel. Improvements in the Civil Service, especially the postal branch. In particular, the improvement of the American and Canadian postal service.

The appointment of female inspectors of factories and workshops. The boarding out of pauper children by parochial boards. There was the question of British Indian subjects deported and imprisoned without trial.

But he campaigned for better business practices also. In one, he pointed to the heavy taxation on patents, saying that someone who had taken out a patent in Britain had to pay so much tax that it was often cheaper to have the product developed in America. Shades of the hovercraft, the vertical take-off aircraft, and the jet engine.

He spoke against the Sugar Bill, which, if introduced, would affect producers of raspberry and strawberry jam and marmalade. Another local-interest battle was against duty on starch and the effect it would have on Dundee's jute industry. Still going on today up to a point is the problem of tuberculosis among cattle, which he raised in 1903.

As an adopted canny Scot he raised the problem of the worn condition of small coins from the previous reign. In 1904, during the reading of the Lighthouses Bill, Leng criticized the government for their parsimony in the upkeep of these essential services.

Several hundred widows of Crimean War soldiers had not received any benefit from the Patriotic Fund established 46 years previously. And in shades of the Iraqi and Afghanistan wars, he fought for consideration of Crimean veterans themselves who were not in receipt of a pension.

Again reflecting affairs which would raise their heads 100 years later he said –
"Having regard to the great expenditure that had taken place during the last few years on great wars and on small wars, some of which were still continuing... if you had been less ready to go into these great enterprises for extending the Empire you would not find the difficulty you now experience in meeting claims which, on their merits, are really irresistible." After a year in Parliament, he addressed a large gathering in the Kinnaird hall. Many women – who did not have the vote – were present. He said that older people who

remembered the Crimean war and the American War of Independence were not in favour of the Boer War. Until he knew the full facts, he was on the side of the Boers. The Colonial Secretary, Chamberlain, was a bully, he said.

He wanted to speak about home rule for Ireland, temperance reform, workmen's compensation, electoral reform, old age pensioners.

In 1902, he originated an interesting debate about the interruption of telegraphic messages through the breakage of overhead cables in storms. He advocated underground cables, or indeed two undersea cables, one down the east coast and one down the west. A similar debate proceeded in 2009 about the proposed power cable between Beauly and Denny. He drew attention to the poor architecture of the new Admiralty offices and one wonders what he would have said about Holyrood.

He also proposed a Standing Order precluding Members voting on Private Bills promoted by companies in which they had an interest. He didn't seem to be successful with this for the practice was still going on in the House of Lords in 2009.

Leng conducted a correspondence with, and raised funds for, Garibaldi the Italian patriot who fought for the unification of his country as a liberal republic, and also against Austrian and French dominance there.

After a very active career at Westminster, he wrote to the chairman of Dundee Liberal Association on 6 February 1905, advising of his intention to retire. The last time he appeared on a political platform was during the General Election in the spring of 1906 at a Liberal rally in the Kinnaird Hall.

He spoke in support of the Liberal candidate so eloquently that a notable citizen was heard to say "What does Sir John want to retire for when he can speak like that ?"

This feeling of adulation was carried on by the quarterly Dundee magazine *The Wasp* whose title betrays its content. It was given to waspish comment upon the town's affairs. At the end of 1901 the editor wrote his thoughts on Leng's Jubilee which took place that year.

"We are glad to find that Dundee's 'Grand Old Man' is about to receive the recognition which merit and worth so richly deserve. Sir John, though possessed of marked gentleness and humility, has proved himself to be a man of remarkable grit, perseverance and ability, combined with laudable ambition. May he long be spared to wear the honours which a grateful and appreciative populace are about to confer on him. Happy is their choice, say we." The Christmas number of *The Wasp* in1901 recorded that Sir John "was presented with his portrait on Friday last by a distinguished representation of ladies and gentlemen.

Sir John's mansion, Kinbrae, which is covered in a following chapter.

Truly he has proved himself an able and efficient citizen, well worthy of the honour."
This portrait is now held in what were the Dundee Art Galleries.

But there is a very different story in *The Wasp* of November 1902.

"Persistent rumours of Sir John Leng's retirement from Parliament have been indignantly
denied. He has absented himself from, and has neglected his duties in a flagrant manner.
The parliamentary session which closed on August 9 lasted about seven months.

"Except for a few days, Sir John was absent in Egypt, and again ran away from his duties
in mid-July. The last month of the session was the most important. Sir John was not
present. He was absent one half of the session altogether. The total number of divisions
was 384. Sir John put in 142.

"As an MP, he should be less vain and egotistical, as an editor he should really 'tak
thought and mend'." How the mighty are fallen, and how short the public memory.

Sir John Leng.
LL.D. D.L. J.P.
EX-M.P. FOR DUNDEE.

CHAPTER 13

JOHN LENG'S TRAVELS - AND HIS DEATH

L ENG was an acute observer of the drift of change and knew that there must be progress and adaptation. To keep himself informed about what was happening elsewhere in the world, he made several fact-finding journeys. These took him to many parts of Europe, to India and Ceylon, and America.

He wrote in detail about his experiences, and much of it appeared in his own daily and weekly publications. Some hard-backed books appeared but I have only been able to locate one, a beautifully-bound volume which is in Dundee's Local History Library. It recounts an 1876 trip to America. Leng's detailed reports of textile factory life in France, Germany, Spain and America are reproduced in the Dundee Year Books of the period, and copies of these are also in the local library. At the time, these articles would be of much interest to Dundee textile manufacturers.

It is surprising that all of the above countries manufactured jute products in large quantities. The working week was 60 hours, except in America where it was 58. Dundee jute workers went to Saxony where they made good money. Workers in Germany were regimented, and in Spain, Leng found very poor conditions and low -level corruption.

He took a trip to India and Ceylon in 1895-6, and wrote several articles about it. Included were The Manchester of India, The Indian Dundee and the Calcutta Jute Mills.

Sir John Leng's first wife, Emily Cook, died in 1892. On 5 June 1897, when he was 69, he married 45-years-old Mary Low, sister of Sir James Low Bt. of Kilmaron, near Cupar, and the first Lord Provost of Dundee. She was born in Kirriemuir in 1852. According to the wording at the Leng Chapel, Mary became John's "faithful partner, cheerful and bright companion of her husband's later years."

Their years together were short. After resigning as an MP, which he did in 1905, Sir John and Lady Leng, together with Miss Leng, set off on a world tour towards the end of 1906. After sailing the Atlantic, they crossed Canada by rail. While in Delmonte, California in early December, what had been taken as severe indigestion became worse. Two members of the family made their way from Dundee to California but arrived too late.

He died there on December 12. He was cremated at Oakland, Calif. and buried at a private service in Vicarsford, Newport. The second Lady Leng survived him by 32 years, dying at Balcairn, Blackness Road, Dundee in 1938.

CHAPTER 14

SIR WILLIAM CHRISTOPHER LENG

THIS gentleman was Sir John's older brother who was also born in Hull, in 1825. He intended to be a lawyer, but a business opportunity presented itself and he became a wholesale chemist.

Although William and John got on well together, they tended to take opposite views on things.

This manifested itself in politics, William eventually turning to being Conservative and John a Liberal. His love of argument led him to the correspondence columns of the Hull Free Press where he advocated sanitary and municipal reform, and the introduction of free libraries. His opponents attempted to vilify him but Leng's wit and sharp pen made his articles the talk of the town.

From time to time, he also wrote pieces for his brother's *Advertiser* and was soon persuaded to come on the staff in Dundee, which he did in 1859. His fellow Dundee journalists found him silent, thoughtful and reflective at work but after he laid his pen down he had the room ringing with laughter. Like his brother, he wrote in the cause of reform. The American civil war was raging and his articles kept *The Advertiser* – almost exclusively among Scottish newspapers - consistently on the side of the North who, of course, triumphed. He surpassed all Scottish writers on maritime matters.

Towards the end of 1864, a friend told William that *The Sheffield Telegraph* was in a poor state but that it had potential and could be bought at a good price. William became managing editor and proprietor. It is said that if he had had gone to London, his skill as an editor would have made him famous nationally.

Because of his writing style, the paper's sales grew rapidly. He took on the Sheffield trade unions which were often seen to be outside the law. He vowed to free the town from their tyranny. The leader columns which he wrote exposed them and things got so sticky at one stage that he took to carrying a revolver. He was accompanied by a policeman wherever he went.

The town was ridden of the terror which it had been under and the Council presented him with his portrait and a purse of 600 sovereigns as a token of thanks.

He was often asked to stand for parliament, and declined. But he was knighted at Queen Victoria's Jubilee in 1888, and chaired many organizations in Sheffield.

The scene switches briefly but explicably to Captain Cook the explorer. Cook had a brother, Thomas who had a son, William. William had five children and one of the daughters, Emily, married John Leng.

One of the sons went to Australia and there he married Ann Stark, originally of Alyth in Perthshire. Ann became widowed and came home to Scotland, landing at Dundee harbour. John Leng sent his brother down to meet her. It was love at first sight and they married in March 1860.

The family home was at Oaklands, Broomhall Park, Sheffield. Sir William died there on 20 February 1902. Ann died in October 1893. They are buried at Eccleshall, Sheffield.

Seymour, home of Sir John's son, John Adam St Quentin Leng.

CHAPTER 15

JOHN ADAM ST QUENTIN LENG

SIR John Leng had two sons and five daughters. The oldest was John Adam St Quentin Leng (1857 – 1937). He was a journalist in the family business, although his name has not shone through. It may have been that he was engaged in some supervisory editorial role. It is significant that even before Sir John went off to be an M.P. he was not one of a group which ran the business. John's name hardly ever appears. In the only picture of him I have seen, and it is rather hazy, he does not look very robust.

In 1898, son John built Seymour, the fine red sandstone house on the river side of Tay Street, Newport and almost under the Tay Road Bridge. From 1949 to 1989, and after it had been sold, it was run as a hotel but is now a nursing home.

Prior to that he lived in another Newport property which he called Seymour House. It was previously called Ashbank and still exists. It is the east-most half of a large semi-detached property immediately east of James Street. The Voters' Roll indicates that he was there from circa 1885 until 1896. When he built the present Seymour he took the name with him and the original is now called Struie Brae.

John married Mary Blyth Johnston. They had three sons. The oldest, also John Adam St Quentin Leng, was killed in action near Arras in 1917.

Then there was Arnold (1896 – 1974). He was educated at Fettes and almost as soon as he left there, was called up to serve in the Great War. Like so many more, the experiences he endured in the trenches left their mark. He had several breakdowns which put him in hospital. He joined the firm on the technical side in 1918. During the general Strike of 1926, he and Howard Thomson delivered *Couriers* to the striking miners – a rather brave thing to do.

In 1933, he and his wife took a small-holding in Hampshire, eventually moving north again to St Andrews. In 1945 they bought The Gorse, a fine house in Barnhill, next to what is now the Woodlands hotel. They had a son John who worked with D.C. Thomson for a time, and Diana, now Mrs Hepburn.

Edward, John's youngest and born in 1903, committed suicide at Seymour in 1945.

The daughters were Mary (1879 – 1953), Dorothy (1888 – 1979), Mildred, who became Mrs. Silver (1891 – 1958) and Hilda (1895 – 1920). Mildred and Dorothy were the last Lengs to live in the house. The "Seymour" Lengs were fine people who were well regarded by their staff.

My mother's bridesmaid was married to Jimmy Mollison who became John Leng's gardener at Seymour. They lived in the little, white-walled, red-roofed cottage by the shore, and just in front of the big house. It's still there today. Originally it had been a salmon bothy, one of several up this stretch of the Tay. The Lengs put in gas during the second world war, and an electric cable was installed by the military to power a red light which was an aid to the Norwegian Catalina flying boats operating from Woodhaven pier. Electricity from that cable was extended to the cottage eventually.

I met up with Jimmy's daughter, Marion, in September 2008 and she gave me a little cameo of life at Seymour.

Arnold Leng

Her father served a gardening apprenticeship with the Dons of Don Brothers Buist, the jute people, at their Broughty Ferry home. After a spell at Balquhidder he moved to Scone Palace where there were 21 people working in the gardens, and 35 in the house. After serving in the Great War, he was with the Marquess of Tweedsdale at Gifford before starting at Seymour in 1931. He had one assistant.

There was a cook, and two maids at Seymour and the Lengs had a low-key life style. Hens were kept and there was a greenhouse with a vine which gave superb grapes. Jimmy was often pruning the vine at ten at night for he felt that everything that went to the big house had to be perfect. The Mollisons were welcome to any surplus. Marion remembers getting Christmas gifts, like a doll or a painting set.

The garage housed three cars. Father John had a Rolls. Dorothy had a big blue open car and one of the other daughters had a grey Riley with red upholstery. There was a chauffeur, Mr Kinnear, who lived with his family in a house within the grounds. His daughter, now Mrs Bunty Doherty, spoke highly of her childhood at Seymour.

As mentioned earlier, John's younger son, Edward who was born in 1903, committed suicide at Seymour in March 1945. The family called him Teddy. He spent several spells in a hospital at Murthly, and never worked. He bought a canoe to use in the river and Jimmy Mollison had to try it out to make sure it wouldn't sink (!) Teddy would visit Mrs Mollison and read to her the poetry of the reclusive Alfred Houseman. These featured unrequited love, grief and death – not the best reading matter for someone of Teddy's disposition.

Teddy's death probably hastened the sale of Seymour. His sisters found that they could not live there. They went to visit their niece, Mrs Baxter, in the Dorking area and liked it there, and bought a large country house. Eventually they bought a flat in the south. At one point, Dorothy was at Buckingham Gate SW1, one of London's better addresses, and just round from Buckingham Palace.

Bank Street, looking towards Barrack Street. Sunlight bathes the Leng buildings and the Kinnaird cinema is prominent.

CHAPTER 16

DR WILLIAM C. LENG

SIR John's second son was William Christopher Leng . Confusing for the researcher, and as we have seen, Sir John had a brother with exactly the same name, and who is the subject of an earlier chapter.

William C. Leng was born in Dundee on 20 July 1859, educated at Dundee High School and in Edinburgh. He married Jessie Millar, the daughter of the minister of Clunie, near Blairgowrie. Around the turn of the 20th century they lived at Redcroft, a most beautiful house in Blackness Road, Dundee. The house is still there, owned by a retired solicitor.

Their next, much larger house, Highfield, was in Newport's Kirk Road.

It was on what is probably the biggest flat piece of land in the burgh. The grounds are extensive and the house faces south over spacious lawns. Inside, it is a little disappointing, ornate Victorian finishings having given way to more minimal Edwardian ones. Highfield is a large house in a fine setting but it is not a grand and extravagant one, in the manner of the Broughty Ferry mansions.

When William decided to build Highfield, it's said that he spent much time looking for a site where he would get the maximum amount of sun. At some point after 1922, he re-named it Waterstone House. He died here on 13 May 1953 and his daughter gifted it to Fife Council as a retirement home. It is called the Leng Home.

As so often happens, a son sometimes has to live in the shadow of a strong-minded and successful father. This seems to have been the case here.

William was 30 when his father, Sir John, was elected MP for Dundee and so had to spend much time in London. Although not the older son, William took a major part in the running of the family publishing business, together with members of the other shareholders' families. The Pattullos were part of the management team. By all accounts, William did the job very well, conducting campaigns for social improvement as his father had done. He wrote many of the leader articles for *The Advertiser*.

He helped establish The Mechanics' Institute, which became Dundee Technical College and is now Dundee Abertay University. He was a senior life governor of University College, now Dundee University, and fought to keep it separate from St Andrews. He was honoured with an LL.D by St Andrews University in 1932.

Dr Leng was associated with Comerton Children's Home, near Newport, and was a member of Newport Boating Club, where his father had been commodore. He was on the board of The Dundee Approved Schools Society. When Dundee became a city in 1889, he was made a J.P.

For most of his life, he was plagued by eye trouble. In 1900, he lost the sight of one eye, and around 1910 he became totally blind. This did not hamper his public activities - indeed he sustained and even increased his interest in current affairs. He did much work for the Dundee Blind Institution, becoming its vice president, and getting for it Royal assent.

His disability did little to restrict his private life. He didn't allow furniture to be moved about, but a maid laid his clothes on the bed and he dressed himself. A secretary read the newspapers to him and he was always au fait with what was going on. He always knew what was in his extensive wine cellar and whether the hedges had been cut straight.

Although he loved the Highlands and enjoyed many holidays on Speyside, he also spent much time in France and the Italian Riviera. He travelled to the office in a chauffeur-driven Rolls Royce, crossing the Tay by the ferry boat.

William Christopher Leng had five daughters - Helen, Lilian, Emily, Ruth and Janet. The latter qualified in medicine and became quite a character, meriting a small chapter which follows.

We are left with the picture of W.C. Leng as a very kind, considerate and mild man who used his considerable wealth to advance the causes of the less fortunate.

CHAPTER 17

DR JANET ELEANOR LENG, R.C.S(ENG)

She was the youngest of Dr William Christopher Leng's five daughters and the only one to make her mark outside the family. She was born on 8 March 1902, the grand-daughter of Sir John Leng. She comes over as an extrovert tom-boy. After the second world war she was turning up for work as an anaesthetist at Dundee Royal Infirmary driving a steely-blue Rolls Royce.

In the 1920s, it was unusual – perhaps even looked at in askance – for the daughter of wealthy parents to have a job. Playing the piano and having genteel conversation during afternoon tea with selected guests were more of the thing. Letters suggest that Janet led a "social" life before the second war, and didn't practice much medicine. She was a very vigorous and intelligent woman, doing well at anything she took up – golf, gardening, bridge.

She had qualified MB.CHb at St Andrews in 1924 and very soon afterwards went off to America where she worked as an osteopath. Later, she did this in Glasgow.

At the outbreak of the second world war, she joined the Royal Army Medical Corps, serving as a major in Northern Ireland, Edinburgh Castle and later in Germany. She took a diploma in anaesthesia at Oxford in 1947 and took the degree of MD at St Andrews in 1950.

During this time, she travelled widely – to Australia, America and also to South Africa where her sister, Mrs Moodie lived. While there, she worked for six months at a mission hospital in the Transkei.

Her base had always been her parents' home at Waterstone, Newport, but after her father's death, she moved to East Stour in Dorset, taking housekeeper and companion, Sarah Martin, with her. Sarah had been table maid at Waterstone.

Restless, she moved back to Scotland in 1983, and an apartment at Bruce Court, Carnoustie. She flew up and down to London frequently. Perhaps Scotland wasn't as she'd remembered and after only a short stay she moved back to a flat in Kensington High Street. From there, she did charity work in homes for the elderly and supported the Anglican church.

She died in London in December 1990, leaving a considerable sum of money to establish the Leng Memorial Trust. (see chapter on The Leng Chapel).

Waterstone House, Newport, home of Dr. William Leng.

CHAPTER 18

OTHER MEMBERS OF THE LENG FAMILY

IN these politically correct times, I hope that I will escape criticism for coming late to Sir John Leng's other daughters. In truth, only one really influences the ongoing story. She is Clara Beatrice who was born in 1865.

She married another Newportonian, William Thomson. William and his brothers David Couper and Frederick were shipowners who also built up one of Britain's most remarkable publishing houses. William and Clara's descendants are running D.C. Thomson & Co today.

Clara died in 1941. For the record, her sisters were Eva (Emily Evangeline, 1854-1930) who married James Sturrock of Forebank Dye Works, Amy (Adeline 1855-1940, Mrs Smith), Elizabeth(1862- 1942, Mrs Stephenson, her husband was a minister) and Harriet who died in infancy.

As has happened with many of the great Dundee dynasties of Victorian times, the line which John Leng created no longer exists in Dundee. In fact, the only male remaining with the Leng surname that I can find is the grandson of the original John Adam St Quentin Leng of Seymour. He is also John Leng, born in 1943, and a bachelor. He lives in Sussex.

John's sister, Mrs Diana Hepburn, lived in Dundee for many years, and she also now lives in Sussex.

Kinbrae (Dundee Public Libraries picture)

CHAPTER 19

KINBRAE

WHEN John Leng arrived in Dundee in 1851, he had little money. But by 1870, he had accrued enough to build the mansion of Kinbrae, just above and to the west of the ferry terminal. It sat between Westwood (Walker, the Dundee jute manufacturer) which was to the east and built around the same time as Kinbrae, and Balmore (Provost Robertson of Dundee, and owner of the Blackness Foundry) to the west.

The house was built by the Perth architect Andrew Heiton (1823- 94). He also built Castleroy in Broughty Ferry whose central hall was "set out like a grand opera." Although Kinbrae looked big from the outside, the accommodation was modest compared to Castleroy, indeed to the neighbouring properties.

In 2009, it was difficult to find someone who had first-hand knowledge of the interior. Fortunately, I was able to renew contact with Mrs Betty Dunn whose father in law owned and lived in the house, and, on his death, willed it to his son. The Dunns, father and son, were associated with the Dundee timber merchants, Melville Dunn. As befits gentlemen, they drove Rolls Royces. One feels that the style which the Dunns could afford to live in would not be dissimilar to the lifestyle of the Lengs.

Betty remembers her first visit to Kinbrae, when she was taken there by her husband-to-be, for "interview" by her future in-laws. On the ground floor, there was a large lounge with a partition. This was kept open in summer when the deep windows afforded views of the superb gardens. In winter, the partition was closed and the family used the smaller portion which had a large and cosy fire and a grand piano. She said there was central heating but it was not very efficient. There was also a pipe organ in this room.

Entering the large front door, which faced south, and passing a cloakroom on the left, one entered a large tiled hall, with an enormous mirror. The walls were panelled, similar to what St Serfs (Westwood) is today.

A wide stair led to a gallery off which were about six bedrooms, two large and the rest modest. There was only one bathroom in the house, but it had a telephone and a walk-in shower which jetted the bather from head to foot. There were additional, small, bedrooms in the towers. I am uncertain about when Kinbrae was vacated by the Leng family, but according to the Dundee street directory, Sir John's second wife was there until 1918-19.

Like Sir John, the Dunns were Liberals, and MPs stayed frequently. Again, as with Sir John,

the house was used for much entertaining. The staff, which numbered around four, lived in the basement.

Mrs Dunn's daughters remember the gardens being huge, with three greenhouses. There was a three-tiered fountain with four decorative swans. There were stables against the south boundary wall, tended by Joe, the Dunn's chauffeur/groom.

Mrs Betty Dunn and her husband John never lived in Kinbrae. By the time they inherited the property, the upkeep would have been enormous and it needed a lot of work to put it in good order. Eventually the house lay empty, the gardens overgrown.

In 1955, it was bought by Newport Town Council who considered it for conversion to housing, or perhaps a hotel. But as happened to so many fine houses at the time, it was demolished - in 1960. A pleasant housing estate now occupies the site. At the top of the road are two big circular stone pillars set in a fine high stone wall which forms the boundary between the houses and the playpark. This is all that remains of Sir John's Kinbrae.

MEMORIAL CHAPEL, VICARSFORD.

This Sanctuary,
for Devotion and Rest and Contemplation,

was dedicated to the Bereaved, the Weary, and the Afflicted,
by Sir John Leng, M.P., of Kinbrae, Newport, A.D. 1897.

CHAPTER 20

THE LENG CHAPEL

TWO miles south east of Newport on Tay and on the left when heading towards St Andrews, stands the Leng Chapel. It was built between 1895 and 1897 by Sir John, in memory of his first wife. She was the first to be buried in what became known as Vicarsford cemetery.

The building is in 13th century French Gothic style, with the private royal chapel of Saint Chapelle, Paris, as the main inspiration. It has a tall green copper roof, and after dark, when it is floodlit, it is a most impressive sight. Leng picked a wonderful site - the views over St Andrews bay and to the Lomonds are spectacular.

The interior is constructed of creamy stone from Caen, in Normandy. The master mason was James Henry White, who was also involved in the construction of the huge St Mary's Cathedral in Palmerston Place in Edinburgh, Mount Stewart House on the Isle of Bute, the restoration of Iona cathedral and various public buildings in St Andrews. The architect was a Dundee man, Thomas Cappon.

Nobody is buried inside the chapel, but Leng graves are around it, particularly on the west side. On the west wall inside is carved an inscription mentioning Sir John's two wives, and on the east wall are the names of the five Newport men who fell in the South African War of 1899-1902. Apart from a dozen or so hand chairs, that is it.

The upkeep and maintenance of the building is funded by The Leng Charitable Trust and it is accessible at certain times. The keyholders are Messrs Thorntons, the Dundee solicitors.

The Leng Charitable Trust is also credited with donating £100,000 to the University of Dundee in 2003 for medical research, and a further £75,000 in 2005 to this University for cardiovascular research. The Trust was set up with money left for this purpose by the granddaughter of Sir John Leng, Dr Janet Leng.

CHAPTER 21

THE SIR JOHN LENG TRUST

AT the time of Sir John Leng's Jubilee in 1901, the public wanted to express their good wishes and thanks for his "50 glorious years" in the city. A public subscription fund was established and donations came from people of all political persuasions, and ordinary townspeople. The result was a portrait by W.Q. Orchardson R.A., which is now in the possession of Dundee City Art Galleries.

Sir John responded by establishing The Sir John Leng Trust in 1902, giving £1500 to establish a fund to "stimulate literary and scientific pursuits among the youth of Dundee and district, and also to encourage and promote the teaching of the songs of Scotland." There was strong accent on Burns material. The original medals were 18 carat gold and supplied by James Ramsay, the Dundee jeweller.

As it stands today, Dundee and district schools are invited to hold a singing competition. The winner receives a silver medal and so is entitled to enter the final of The Leng Medal competition. For this, there is a gold medal for one boy and one girl. The competition is the envy of other towns in Scotland. Most years, there are around 40 female and 10 male entrants. The standard among many is professional. The songs may be of Burns origin, or they may be modern, so long as they are Scots. The competition was extended to include Newport, Tayport, Monifieth and Carnoustie.

There is still an essay competition too, although it is less well supported. It is referred to nowadays as "The Book Prize." It is presented each year in each of the Senior Secondary schools to the best pupil in Sixth Year in Science or English, at the discretion of the Rector.

The first essay competition was won by Bella Brand of Benvie Road, Dundee, who was a student at Dundee University College. Having been at Hawkhill and Blackness schools, she won a bursary to the Harris where she was dux. A further bursary got her to the College. A bright girl, I wonder what became of her.

The first Leng Medal competition for singing was held in the Kinnaird Hall, and was won by Lizzie Mill of Liff Road School. Sir John and Lady Leng received the Silver Medal winners in the *Advertiser* office on Christmas Eve and presented each with a book of Scots songs.

In 1943, the government prohibited the making of medals. Gold medal winners were given Savings Certificates and Silver winners, a framed certificate. Later, the awarding of medals was reinstated.

The Trust, whose Clerk is Mr Donald Gordon of Blackadders, the Dundee law firm, is now run by governors nominated by Dundee University, directors of the High School, the Director of Education, and the directors of D.C. Thomson and Co.

Looking east down Bank Street, before the demolition of Barrack Street. Neish and Patullo's offices would be at the far end on the left.

CHAPTER 22

JAMES PATTULLO AND WILLIAM NEISH

IT would be fitting to include a small chapter on the two men who brought John Leng to Dundee in 1851.

James Pattullo was born at Baldragon in the parish of Strathmartine in 1818. He served a law apprenticeship in Dundee and rounded it off at Edinburgh University. Soon after returning to Dundee in 1844, he went into partnership with William Neish, and this lasted for 11 years, after which Neish went off to become a member of the English Bar.

In 1857, Pattullo assumed as a partner, Thomas Thornton – later Sir Thomas – whose name lives on in Dundee legal circles. This lasted until 1881 when Pattullo assumed his nephew, Henry A. Pattullo as a partner, the business continuing for many years as J. and H. Pattullo.

In 1867, he bought the estate of Persey, in Glenshee, eight miles north of Blairgowrie, on the west side of the road. In the following year, he bought the adjoining estate of Ashmore, on the east side of the Glenshee road. The house is magnificent and at the time of writing is owned by a Swiss businessman who keeps it beautifully. Later, the estate of South Persey was added. His Dundee home was Abertay, Monifieth Road, Broughty Ferry.

Pattullo became deeply interested in agriculture and in his later years, farmed the estates himself. He also dedicated himself to public service. He died in 1904 and is buried in the Western Cemetery, Dundee. He left five sons and two daughters. One of the sons, Norman, was on the management side of the Leng business for many years.

William Neish was a member of a remarkable family. His father was a merchant and manufacturer in Dundee. The family owned The Laws and Omachie farms at Newbigging. Neish qualified as a Writer at Edinburgh and returning to Dundee, went into partnership with Pattullo.

In 1856, he bought the estate of Easter Clepington from Mr R.H. Arklay which comprised a huge greenfield site extending west from the present Arklay Street. At the time, people thought he was mad. But just think. Jute was expanding rapidly and land was needed to build mills on. More mills meant more people. More people meant more sales of *The Advertiser* in which Neish was a major shareholder. The money was rolling in.

In 1871, he bought the estate of Tannadice, near Finavon in Angus (hence Tannadice Park, home of Dundee United which was on Easter Clepington ground). By way of a pleasant occupation, he became a barrister at Lincoln's Inn. He had a London town house, and property in the Isle of Wight. Eventually he sold up in the south and took up residence in the fine mansion house at Tannadice, which is still there and in good order.

He gave generously and anonymously to many causes in Dundee, including the erection of St Paul's and St Salvador's churches. He had two daughters and six sons who all left healthy wills.

The Neish story does not end there. Captain James Neish built Fort William House in West Ferry. It is now the home of the Royal Tay Yacht Club. Captain Neish was responsible for repeatedly bringing jute samples from Calcutta to Dundee. A relative, Thomas Neish persevered in trying to get the fibres to cling together. He succeeded, using whale oil and water, as we now know. Thomas Neish became known as the father of the jute industry. As far as I know, and like the Lengs, there are no members of the Neish family left in Dundee.

But there are Pattullos all over the Howe of Strathmore, farming the fine soil. The last survivor of James Pattullo's own line, Ian Pattullo, born in 1963, lives in Vancouver.

Some members of the Neish and Pattullo families, through their connection with John Leng and Co, remain shareholders in D.C. Thomson & Co Ltd.

Sir John Leng.

At the back of this Thomson family group are Clara(Leng) and William Thomson 3rd. The old man is William Thomson 2nd, shipowner and eventually publisher, who lived modestly in Newport. Holding the younger child (Sidney) of William and Clara is William 2nd's sister, Johan. The older child is William Harold Thomson who became company chairman after D.C. Thomson. The picture was taken in 1889.

CHAPTER 23

IN CONCLUSION

JOHN Leng was a man of parts and he excelled in most of them. He was a fine journalist who established a rapport with his readers who were, in the main, the working people of Scotland. He gave them what they wanted. Radicalism which supported the social change which the people desired. Most of the social causes which he fought for came to pass eventually.

In a careful and planned way, he turned *The Advertiser* into one of the best newspapers in Scotland, and also established Dundee as the centre of journalism north of the border. Once *The Advertiser* was firmly on its feet, he launched *The People's Journal* in the same planned and considered way. It became the biggest selling weekly outside London. From that, he launched *The People's Friend*, still going strong, and the oldest women's magazine in the English-speaking world.

Leng was an innovator. He was always at the front of newspaper technology. He installed the best of equipment and replaced it regularly. This took money, lots of it. So he was also a good business man. He had connections and contacts at all levels of society and was hugely popular. He was an engaging man who could inspire people around him, and he could get things done.

From all reports, he was a kindly and generous man, really interested in the welfare and happiness of his staff. His top men, the editors and senior journalists, remained with him and were loyal to the principles he laid down. But the Leng family did not continue to successfully run the empire in Sir John's old age. The firm became ripe for a take-over.

The reason is simple. John Leng was a one-off. Looking back, it seems quite plain that there was not one person left in the business who had all his qualities. Quite apart from business acumen, and just as important in the unique world that is journalism, creative talent is paramount.

Good editors fly publications by the seat of their pants. It is a touchy feely quality, and they are born with it. It is not possible to make a creative journalist. When they retire, or give up the helm, very often these people are irreplaceable.

John Leng's hand had been virtually off the day-to-day tiller since 1889 when he was 61, because of his parliamentary duties. After that, the business was in the control of his son, the blind Dr William Leng and a few of the Pattullos. They were probably able enough men, but they were not of the same stamp as the multi-talented Sir John.

In 1905, barely a hundred yards away was the headquarters of the burgeoning D.C. Thomson & Co Ltd who had only become actively involved in publishing in 1884. William Thomson (2nd) who came to Dundee in 1838 from Pittenweem and opened a clothier's shop in Reform Street also became very successful through shipping.

Further, he lent regular sums to the financially-fragile *Courier*. When this went bust in 1884, William found himself the major creditor and fell heir to the paper. He had little idea how to run it and asked his second son, David Coupar Thomson to help. The eldest son William(3rd) was a financial man and he kept a watching brief. The youngest son, Frederick, also came into the business.

These were very able men, each playing his part in developing the family businesses and interests. Despite the great rivalries between the Thomson and Leng families, I strongly suspect, there was respect for each other at the time. William(3rd) married Sir John Leng's daughter Clara in 1886. This must have had a bearing in the take-over of the Leng business by D.C. Thomson & Co in 1905.

At that point, the Thomson brothers were in their prime – William was 45, David was 44 and Frederick, 41. The following year they would open their state-of-the art offices at Meadowside.

Dr William C. Leng was 46, not in the best of health, and he must have felt pretty isolated. We will never know the whole story of the take-over. The present Thomson firm holds no records concerning the Lengs, and the main part (two thirds) of the take-over occurred over 100 years ago.

It seems that it was a simple case of the strong gobbling up the weak. Having said that, there is a feeling among some of the present day Thomson family that, at the time, both the Thomson and Leng sets of publications were not doing particularly well and a take-over was a "must". Eventually, *The Courier* would kill *The Advertiser* and *The Telegraph* would kill *The Post*.

The union between William(3rd) and Clara Leng was a most important one. It produced the family line which runs the Thomson business to this day. From D.C. Thomson and his brothers onwards, the directors have been shrewd and able businessmen who are have been present in depth. As ex-chairman Mr W. Harold Thomson is reputed to have said of his two sons, Brian and Derek, then joint managing directors - "The boys know what is going on." They certainly did.

ADDENDUM

LIST OF THE ADVERTISER EDITORS

1801 – James Roger
1801 – 1809 –James Saunders
1809 – 1825 – Robert Stephen Rintoul
1825 – 1835 – John Galletly
1835 – 1840 – Peter Brown
1840 – 1842 – James McDonald Saunders (son of James Saunders)
1842 – 1851 – Francis W. Baxter
1851 – John Austin Lake Gloag
1851 – 1901 – John Leng (Knighted 1893)
1894 – 1901 – T. Carlaw Martin (acting editor)
1901 – July 1910 – T. Carlaw Martin (Knighted 1909)
July 1910 – May 1926 – Alex Urquhart

In May 1926, at the time of the General Strike, *The Dundee Courier* and
The Dundee Advertiser amalgamated under the title of *The Courier and Advertiser*.

LIST OF THE PEOPLE'S JOURNAL EDITORS

January 1858 - December 1860   John Leng
December 1860 - December 1898 William D.Latto
December 1898 – December 17 1905. Editors in this period cannot be traced.
December 18 1905 – March 9 1905 D.L. Cromb
March 1909 – June 1910 James Fairlie
June 1910 – February 1912 William Blackwood
March 1912 – March 31, 1950 George G.Glass
April1 1950 – April 28 1973 James B. Hood
April 1973 – December 17 1977 Donald B. Coutts
December 18 1977 – 1990 (closure) Robert Paterson.

ACKNOWLEDGEMENTS

I would like to thank the following -

John Irvine of the Tay Valley Family History Society.

Mrs Betty Dunn and her two daughters, Maureen and Valerie, re Kinbrae.

Mrs Diana Hepburn (nee Leng) for her interest and support.

The ladies of the Dundee Local History Library.

Aberdeen Local Studies Library re Donside Mills.

Bob Benzies re The Leng Chapel.

Stuart Cameron for the cover design.

Moira Gaffney for the layout of the book.

Andrew F. Thomson (Chairman), Christopher H. W. Thomson and L. Murray Thomson, directors of D.C. Thomson & Co Ltd for their most generous offer to print the book. In return, I am pleased to give them the copyright to use as they see fit in the future. I also wish them all the best in all their endeavours, as guardians of a remarkable family firm.

*Wherever possible, I have made every effort to trace the owners of the pictures used in the book, and to credit them. If I have failed with any of them, I offer my apologies.